THOMAS HAMILTON MURRAY.

Irish Rhode Islanders in the American Revolution

WITH SOME MENTION OF THOSE SERVING IN THE REGIMENTS OF ELLIOTT, LIPPITT, TOPHAM, CRARY, ANGELL, OLNEY, GREENE, AND OTHER NOTED COMMANDERS

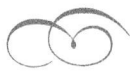

Thomas Hamilton Murray
Secretary-General, American-Irish Historical Society

HERITAGE BOOKS
2012

HERITAGE BOOKS
AN IMPRINT OF HERITAGE BOOKS, INC.

Books, CDs, and more—Worldwide

For our listing of thousands of titles see our website
at
www.HeritageBooks.com

A Facsimile Reprint
Published 2012 by
HERITAGE BOOKS, INC.
Publishing Division
100 Railroad Ave. #104
Westminster, Maryland 21157

Originally published:
Providence, R.I.
The American-Irish Historical Society
1903

— Publisher's Notice —
In reprints such as this, it is often not possible to remove blemishes from the original. We feel the contents of this book warrant its reissue despite these blemishes and hope you will agree and read it with pleasure.

International Standard Book Numbers
Paperbound: 978-0-7884-0794-9
Clothbound: 978-0-7884-9238-9

IRISH RHODE ISLANDERS IN THE AMERICAN REVOLUTION.

THE Irish chapter in American history possesses great interest. The chapter is an essential one, and deserves careful attention, earnest study and high respect. The Irish element forms a basic part of the American people. Consequently, a knowledge of this part is necessary to the proper understanding of the origin, growth and integration of that people.

We can, as Americans, pursue this study very profitably. We may begin the Irish chapter back in the sixth or the seventh century with the reputed advent on these shores of the Irish Brendan.[1] Or if we prefer for the time to waive that tradition, we may start at 1620 and the *Mayflower*.

Rev. William Elliot Griffis, in his work *Brave Little*

[1] See De Roo's *History of America Before Columbus* (Philadelphia, Pa., J. B. Lippincott Co., 1900). A work of extraordinary interest and value.

Webb's *Compendium of Irish Biography* (Dublin, 1878).

O'Donoghue's *Brendaniana. St. Brendan the Voyager, in Story and Legend* (Dublin, 1893).

La Navigatio Sancti Brendani. Edita ed illustrata da Francesco Novati (Bergamo, Cattaneo, 1892).

Voyages (Les) Merveilleux de Saint Brandan à la Recherche du Paradis terreste. Avec introduction par Francisque-Michel (Paris, 1878).

Gustav Schirmer's *Zur Brendanus-Legende. Probevorlesung über Irlands Antheil an der Englischen Literatur* (Leipzig, 1888).

Joyce's *History of Ireland* (London, 1893).

Note to Otway's *Sketches in Erris and Tyrawley* (Dublin, 1845).

North Ludlow Beamish's *The Discovery of America by the Northmen in the Tenth Century, with Notices of the Early Settlements of the Irish in the Western Hemisphere* (London, 1841).

Holland and what She Taught Us (Boston and New York, 1894), says on page 208: "In the *Mayflower* . . . were one hundred and one men, women, boys and girls as passengers, besides captain and crew. These were of English, Dutch, French, and Irish ancestry, and thus typical of our national stock." Plymouth was founded in 1620. William Bradford, who became governor of the colony, has left a manuscript history of the plantation. This history was recently (Boston, 1898) issued in printed form by the state of Massachusetts. In it is mentioned the arrival at Plymouth colony in 1626-'27 of a ship with a large number of passengers on board. Bradford says: "The cheefe amongst these people was one M^r. Fells and M^r. Sibsie, which had many servants belonging unto them, many of them being Irish."

Irish names are found in Virginia as early as 1621. Doubtless there were Irish among the passengers who, in 1630, came to "the Bay" in the ships with John Winthrop. Indeed, Winthrop in his *Journal* specifically refers to an Irishman—Field—who was at that time, or soon after, a member of the colony. Capt. Daniel Patrick is believed to have been an Irishman. One historical writer states that his surname was originally Gillpatrick, and that he had gone over to Holland where he followed a military career, and eventually married a Dutch wife.

We know from Hotten's *Original Lists* and other authorities that Irish emigration to Virginia was in progress as far back as 1634-'35. There were Irish in Maryland at as early a period. Many Irish pioneers were in the West Indies at the same time. A list of people in Barbadoes,[1] in 1638, who then possessed more than ten acres of land each, contains a number of typically Irish names. We know that William Collins[2] led a number of Irish refugees, about 1640, to Connecticut from the West Indies. There were Irish Catholics in New York in 1642. Settlers bearing Irish names are found in Rhode Island in Roger Williams' day. On his return from England, in 1644, Williams brought letters to "leading men of the Bay" in which Irish comers to America are mentioned. The great Irish revolt against England in 1641, and the preceding and succeeding wars exiled thousands of Irish Catholics. Exodus followed exodus during Cromwell's barbarous career. These facts indicate that Irish immigration to the American colonies had, at that period, already attained large proportions.

In 1652 Cromwell's commissioners in Ireland recommended[3] that "Irish women as being too numerous now . . . be sold to merchants and transported to Virginia, New England, Jamaica, or other countries." The recommendation was carried out. In 1653 Captain John Vernon contracted with Messrs. Sellick and Leader for 250 women of the Irish nation and 300 Irish men, "to transport them into New England." These were to be secured in the country within twenty miles of Cork, Youghal and Kinsale, Waterford and Wexford.

Bruodin[4] expresses the opinion that over 100,000 Irish

[1] Narragansett *Historical Register*.
[2] Felt's *Ecclesiastical History of New England*.
[3] See Prendergast's *Cromwellian Settlement of Ireland;* Thebaud's *Irish Race in the Past and Present;* Condon's *Irish Race in America;* Cullen's *Story of the Irish in Boston;* Walpole's *History of the Kingdom of Ireland;* Thomas D'Arcy McGee's *History of Early Irish Settlers in North America*.
[4] *Propuguaculum* (Pragæ anno 1669), quoted in Condon's *Irish Race in America*.

were then obliged to leave their native land. According to a letter in Dr. Lingard's possession, fully 60,000 Irish people of both sexes were transported in a single year, 1656. These are but a few instances of many conditions and causes under which and for which the Irish early came not only to New England, Pennsylvania, Virginia, and neighboring colonies, but also to the islands of the West Indies.

The accession of Charles II did not stem the tide of Irish immigration which has continued to this day. They came then, as they come now, from every province in Ireland—from Ulster, Leinster, Munster, and Connacht. The period of King Philip's war, 1675-'76, found many Irish throughout New England. The writer recently compiled a list of Irish [1] soldiers who fought in that war in defense of the colonies, and the material was then by no means exhausted. From 1676 to 1776, a period of one hundred years, great waves of Irish immigration, closely following each other, came to the American colonies. A large part of these sturdy people who thus came to our shores were Roman Catholics, due credit being given a host of Irish Protestants who also fled the old land with their Catholic fellow-countrymen.

At this late day no argument is necessary to sustain

[1] *The Irish Soldiers in King Philip's War* (*Rosary Magazine*, New York city, March, 1896). A number of soldiers bearing Irish names came to Rhode Island during Philip's war (1675-'76), from Connecticut and the "Bay." They included: James Murphy, Daniel Tracy, Edward Larkin, John Roach, James Welch and John Casey. Murphy, Tracy, Larkin, Roach and Welch are all believed to have been from Connecticut. Casey was from what is now the town of Brookline, Mass., then called Muddy River. He was wounded in the "Great Swamp fight." Roach was subsequently given, as a gratuity, by the town of Norwalk, Conn., a tract of land "consisting of twelve acres more or less laid out upon the west side of the West Rock, so called." In the Norwalk records, he is spoken of as a soldier in the "Direful Swamp Fight."

the assertion that the triumph of our Revolution was in a large measure due to the Irish who bore arms in the cause of liberty. This has been amply testified to by Washington, Lee, Franklin, Custis and a host of other eminent authorities. In England similar testimony has been given by Galloway, Robertson, Mountjoy and a number of other well-informed personages.

EARLY IRISH SETTLERS IN RHODE ISLAND.

Many Irish settled in Rhode Island long before the Revolution.[1] In addition to those arriving from Connecticut and the "Bay," others undoubtedly landed, direct from the Old Country, at Providence, Newport and other points. In his researches, the writer has found the following typically Irish names in Rhode Island as early as the period mentioned in each case:

Larkin, 1655; Dunn, 1655; Casey, 1663; Kelly, 1669; Macoone, 1669; Heffernan, 1671; Martin, 1677; Macarte (MacCarthy),[2] 1677; Long, 1677; Devett, 1685; Malavery, 1687; Dailey, 1689; Linniken, 1690; Cary, 1693; Dring, 1696; Doyle, 1698; Higgins, 1699; Moore, 1700; Walch, 1703; Mitchell, 1703; Coursey, 1713; Murphy, 1718; Lawless, 1720; Carty, 1721; Mackown, 1723; O'Harra, 1728; Phelon, 1730; Shay, 1731; Joyce, 1731; Conner, 1732; Casside (Cassidy), 1732; Gallagher, 1736; Lyon, 1737; Mackey, 1737; Hurley, 1740; McCane, 1740; Sullivan, 1740; Whelen, 1740-'41; McGonegal, 1742; Delaney, 1742; Farrell, 1742; Mulholland, 1742; Rourk, 1742; Dempsey, 1743;

[1] The names of many of them may be found in Arnold's *Vital Record of Rhode Island*.
[2] See pamphlet on *Charles McCarthy, A Rhode Island Pioneer*, 1677, by Thomas Hamilton Murray (Somerset, O., 1901).

Fitzgerald, 1743; Hanley, 1745; Egan, 1745; McDonald, 1745; Donnelly, 1747; Tally, 1747; Byrn, 1747; Lanahan, 1750; Maguire, 1750; O'Brien, 1751; Donovan, 1751; Barrett, 1751; Cavenaugh, 1752; Flynn, 1752; Murray, 1752; Hickey, 1752; Hartagan, 1753; McMullen, 1754; Bourk, 1755; Dwyer, 1756; O'Neil, 1756; Ryan, 1756; Magee, 1758; Donohoe, 1758; Sheehan, 1759; Hearn, 1759; McGrath, 1759; Mullen, 1760; Gorman, 1761; Lary, 1761; Dermott, 1761; Fitzpatrick, 1761; Dunphy, 1765; Carroll, 1768; Roach, 1773; Mahoney, 1774; Rohan, 1774. It is quite probable that some of the foregoing names are found in Rhode Island even at earlier periods.

RHODE ISLAND EARLY RESISTS BRITISH OPPRESSION.

Rhode Island was among the first of the colonies to resent British oppression. In 1765 she vigorously opposed the Stamp Act and denied the right of any power but her own General Assembly to levy taxes on the colony. In 1766 a liberty tree was dedicated in Newport. In 1768 a like event took place in Providence.

During the next year a British revenue sloop was attacked at Newport. In June, 1772, another British vessel, the armed revenue schooner *Gaspee*, was attacked some miles below Providence, by a patriotic expedition from the latter place, and destroyed. Her commander was wounded and Dr. Henry Sterling, an Irish surgeon of Providence, was called[1] to attend him. Deputy Governor Darius Sessions writing to Governor Wanton, under date of Providence, June 12, 1772, relative to the attack on the

[1] Dr. Mawney is also mentioned in this respect.

Gaspee, says: "P. S. Dr. Sterling, who attends Capt. Dudingston, informed us yesterday that he was in a fair way to recover of his wounds." In 1775 James Black, partner of Alexander Black, an Irishman and leading merchant, was a member of the committee of inspection for Providence, appointed to maintain trade on an equitable basis.

At the outbreak of the Revolution the Irish in Rhode Island were not only numerous but included people of weight and influence. They did much toward fanning the flames of patriotism.

Events moved rapidly. Washington visited Providence in April, 1776. On May 4 of that year the Assembly formally renounced allegiance to Great Britain. This was two months before the general Declaration of Independence at Philadelphia.

The number of troops[1] enlisted from Rhode Island during the War of the Revolution was as follows: In 1775, 1,193 men; in 1776, 1,900; in 1777, 2,048; in 1778, 3,056; in 1779, 1,263; in 1780, 915; in 1781, 464; in 1782, 481; in 1783, 372.

KNOX AND SULLIVAN IN THE STATE.

At least two generals of Irish parentage were prominently identified with Rhode Island during the Revolution. They were Henry Knox and John Sullivan. Knox was born in Boston, Mass., and became a member of the Charitable Irish Society of that city, an organization of which his father was a founder. The General also belonged to

---

[1] From the American Almanac, quoted in the R. I. State Manual. Some Rhode Island authorities hold that the number of enlistments was larger than here given.

the Friendly Sons of St. Patrick, of Philadelphia.[1] Sullivan was the son of an Irish schoolmaster.[2] The latter's name was at one time O'Sullivan, and in the old land the clan had fought English oppression for centuries. It was eminently fitting that an American scion of the family should be found opposing the same power that had persecuted his Irish forefathers.

Knox, then a colonel, was in Rhode Island in April, 1776. At the request of Governor Cooke he planned defenses for Newport, of which the governor informed Washington[3] in the following letter: "I prevailed upon Colonel Knox who passed through this town [Providence], on his way to Norwich, to take a view of Newport, and to direct such works to be thrown up as he should think necessary for the defence of the place. He is clearly of opinion that the town of Newport may be secured; and hath left some directions, which I have ordered to be carried into execution. They have begun the works, and I believe will this day complete a battery which commands the north entrance of the harbor. To-morrow they begin the fortifications upon Fort Island; and if it be in our power to complete the works, I have no doubt it will put a total end to toryism in this colony."

[1] Quite a number of patriots who attained eminence during the Revolution belonged to Irish organizations. Thus, Hon. Thomas McKean, a signer of the Declaration of Independence, was the first president of the Hibernian Society, of Philadelphia; Stephen Moylan, the distinguished soldier, was the first president of the Friendly Sons of St. Patrick, Philadelphia; "Mad Anthony" Wayne belonged to both these societies, as did also John Barry, the famous naval officer. Other members of the Friendly Sons of St. Patrick, Philadelphia, or of the Hibernian Society of that city were: Gen. Richard Butler, Gen. Edward Hand, Gen. William Irvine, Gen. Walter Stewart, Gen. William Thompson, Col. John Nixon, Col. Sharp Delaney, Col. Charles Stewart, Col. John Patton, Lieut. Col. George Latimer, Lieut. Col. Thomas Robinson and many other gallant men of the Revolutionary period.

[2] Thomas C. Amory's *Master Sullivan of Berwick.*

[3] Drake's *Memoir of Henry Knox.*

Knox's letter to Washington concerning the foregoing incident, was as follows:

"NORWICH, 21 April, 1776.

" In passing through Providence, Governor Cooke and a number of the principal people were very pressing for me to take Newport on my way, in order to mark out some works for that place. . . . Knowing your excellency's anxiety for the preservation of every part of the continent, I conceived it to be my duty to act in conformity to your wishes, especially as I could get to Norwich as soon as the stores which set out on the 14th. Accordingly I went to Newport, and marked out five batteries, which from the advantageous situation of the ground, must, when executed, render the harbor exceedingly secure. . . ."

Knox also visited Rhode Island at other times. He speaks of being entertained at Newport by the French officers, including Count Rochambeau, the Counts Deux Ponts, Gen. Chastellux, Marquis Laval, and others. He mentions especially Chastellux " at whose *petits soupers* I was invited two evenings out of three during when at Newport."

SULLIVAN TAKES COMMAND IN THE STATE.

Sullivan took command of the Rhode Island department in 1778, conducted the siege of Newport,[1] commanded in the subsequent battle and remained in the state until late in March, 1779. Under him at the battle on the island were also his brothers, James[2] and Eben. His forces included many officers and men of Irish lineage.

[1] Amory's *Life of Major-General John Sullivan.*
[2] Amory's *Life of Governor James Sullivan.*

Upon the declaration of independence in Rhode Island, the courts of law had been declared to be no longer considered as the king's courts. It was forbidden under heavy penalties to pilot any of the king's ships in Rhode Island waters. It was decreed by the General Assembly "That if any person within this State shall, under pretence of praying or in any other way and manner whatever, acknowledge or declare the said King to be our Lord and Sovereign, or shall pray for the success of his arms, . . . shall be deemed guilty of a high misdemeanor." The penalty provided was a fine of £100 and all the costs of prosecution. On May 3, 1775, Governor Joseph Wanton, who was of strong Tory proclivities, was suspended by the General Assembly of Rhode Island, and on Nov. 7, 1775, he was formally deposed.

The Irish element—and by this the writer means those of Irish descent as well as of Irish birth—was handsomely represented in the forces raised by the infant state. The following list of Irish Rhode Islanders who rendered patriotic service in civic, military, or naval spheres during the Revolution illustrates this. Some of the Rhode Island forces did duty as State troops, others as Continentals.

The list here presented has been compiled only after careful research and investigation. If by accident, however, any names appear here that should not, the writer is convinced that they are more than counterbalanced by names which might be included, but which are not, owing to want of distinctiveness. Thus, without question, there were many Irish Rhode Islanders whose names are not sufficiently typical to indicate their Hibernian origin. There were probably scores of such, which, if added to this roll, would greatly extend it.

The authorities consulted in the preparation of the list have been many. They include muster and size rolls of the Revolution, records of the General Assembly, official war correspondence, company and regimental reports, and other equally authoritative sources. The large manuscript volumes in the possession of Rhode Island's secretary of state have been examined, and so, too, has the card index in the office of the R. I. Record Commissioner. Use has also been made of that valuable work, Cowell's *Spirit of '76 in Rhode Island*. Material has also been received from Miss Virginia Baker, author of *The History of Warren, Rhode Island, In the War of the Revolution*. Mr. Edward Field's work, *Revolutionary Defences in Rhode Island*, has been consulted, as have Bicknell's *History of Barrington, R. I.*, and like publications.

SOME RHODE ISLANDERS IN THE REVOLUTION.

Bagley, Dennis
Barns, Mark
Barr, Matthew
Barrett, Daniel
Barritt, John
Barry, John
Bennett, Edward
Bennett, James
Bennett, Joseph
Bennett, Matthew
Bishop, James
Black, James
Black, Samuel
Boyd, Andrew
Bryan, James
Bryan, Matthew
Buckley, Charles
Burk, David
Burk, John
Burk, Tobias
Burke, Edward
Burke, Joseph
Burke, Timothy
Burn, Benjamin
Burns, Peter
Burns, Thomas
Burns, Walter
Burns, William
Butler, James
Butler, John
Cain, Andrew
Cane, Jeremiah
Capron, Patrick
Carrell, John
Carroll, Joseph
Carey, Thomas

Cary, Michael
Cary, William
Casey, Edward
Casey, James
Casey, John
Caton, Patrick
Cavan, Francis
Clarke, Barney
Clarke, Lawrence
Conley, John
Conner, Thomas
Connor, Edward
Conway, John
Cooney, Michael
Corkern [Corcoran?], Morris
Cowen, John
Cowen, Peter
Cowen, Stephen
Creed, William
Crou, William
Dailey, James
Dailey, Peter
Daily, James
Daily, Stephen
Daley, Peter
Dawley, Daniel
Dawley, Michael
Day, Peter
Doherty, Michael
Donal, James
Donnelly, Edward
Donovan, Pierce
Doolinty, Philip
Dorrance, Alex.
Dorrance, George
Dorrance, George, Jr.
Dorrance, John
Dougherty, Michael

Dougherty, Thomas
Dowd, Daniel
Doyle, Luke
Driskel, Philip, Jr.
Driskel, William
Driskill, Cornelius
Driskill, John
Driskil, Philip
Driskill, Richard
Dunn, Samuel
Dunphy, Patt
Duyer [or Dwyer], Patrick
Eagan, Robert
Ennis, William
Fee, William
Fitzgerald, Edward
Fitzgerald, Patten
Fitzgerrald, Gerrald
Flanagan, James
Forde, Joseph
Foster, James
Foy, Patrick
Gaffery, Joseph
Galligher, Bernard
Garey, Thomas
Gibbons, John
Gleeson, Thomas
Griffen, James
Griffin, Anthony
Griffin, John
Griffin, Philip
Hackett, Benjamin
Hackmet, Patrick
Hagerty, Cornelius
Haney, John
Hanley, Matthew
Hannington, Patrick
Hany, James

Harrington, Patrick
Harrington, Richard
Hart, Matthew
Hart, Nicholas
Hayden, James
Hayden, Richard
Hayes, James
Healy, David
Hendly, Matthew
Herrick, Martin
Hervey, Edward
Hervey, William
Hickey, John
Hickey, Patrick
Hicks, Barnabas
Hogan, Dennis
Hogen, John
Hughes, Thomas
Huzzey, John
Jackson, Bartholomew
Jackson, Benjamin
Jackson, Daniel
Jackson, Thomas
Joyce, Alfred
Joyce, John
Kelley, Daniel
Kelley, Eleazer
Kelley, Erasmus
Kelley, Joseph
Kelley, Michael
Kelley, Thomas
Kelley, William
Kelly, Charles
Kelly, David
Kelly, Duncan
Kelly, Eseck
Kelly, John
Kelly, Oliver

Kelly, Stephen
Kelly, Timothy
Kelly, William
Kenady, Hugh
Kennady, Robert
Kennedy, John
Killey, John
Killey, Michael
Killey, Stephen
King, James
Kirby, John
Knox, James
Larkin, John
Larkin, Timothy
Lawless, John
Lawless, William
Lemasny, Daniel
Long, Stephen
Long, Thomas
Lowery, James
Lyon, Daniel
Mackay, M.
Madden, James
Mahony, John
Mahony, Timothy
Malone, William
Maloney, Thomas
Manning, Joseph
Martin, Jeremiah
McAfferty, Charles
McBride, Alexander
McCaffray, Matthew
McCall, William
McCartee, Dennis
McCartel, Dennis
McCarthy, Ensign
McCarthy, John
McCarthy, Timothy

McCavney, Francis
McCloud, John
McCowan, Hugh
McCoy, William
McDermot, Barnabus
McDonald, Charles
McDonnold, Hugh
McDonnold, John
McGowan, John
McGrath, Edward
McKown, Patrick
McLaughlin, John
McLouth, Lawrence
McMillen, Charles
McMillen, Peter
McMillion, Joseph
McMillion, Peter
McMilon, Joseph
McMullan, Patrick
McNamara, Patrick
M'Carty, William
M'Case, James
M'Clanen, John
Meloney, Thomas
Miller, Daniel
Mitchell, James
Mitchell, John
Mitchell, Thomas
Mitchell, William
Monks, Daniel
Moore, Christopher
Moore, John
Moore, Michael
Moore, William
Moran, Joseph
Morrigan, Michael
Morris, Edward
Morris, Peter

Morrison, Peter
Mullen, Charles
Mulligan, Edward
Mulligan, Francis
Murfee, Edward
Murfey, Edward
Murphy, John
Murphy, Martin
Murray, Anthony
Murray, John
Murray, Thomas
Murrey, Joseph
Nagle, Arthur
Nagle, Peter
Noonen, John
Norton, Joseph
Obrian, Elizabeth
O'Brian, John M.
O'Brian, Patrick
O'Briant, William
O'Brien, William
O'Bryan, William
O'Daniel, Manie
O'Harra, Geo.
O'Kelley, John
O'Neal, John
Parker, William
Patrick, James
Powers, Edward
Powers, Thomas
Ragen, John
Ray, Stephen
Ray, Thomas
Read, James
Read, Joseph
Read, Oliver
Ready, Stephen
Reynolds, James

Reynolds, Thomas
Ryand [Ryan], John
Reily, Terence
Riley, John
Ross, Edward
Shields, Richard
Smith, John
Sterling, Henry
Sullivan, Cornelius,
Sullivan, Daniel
Sullivan, John
Sullivan, William
Tracy, John

Tracy, Patrick
Tuley, John
Wall, Daniel
Watson, Charles
Welch, James
Welch, John
Welch, John, 2d
Whalen, Jeremiah
Whalen, Joseph
Whellon, Richard
Wilson, John
Wright, Michael

IRISH NAMES, TYPICAL AND OTHERWISE.

It is, of course, possible that a few of the foregoing may not have been of Irish birth or extraction. The greater part of those mentioned in the list, however, undoubtedly were. We know, for instance, that James Bishop, William Parker, Henry Sterling, John Wilson, Daniel Monks, and Charles Watson were natives of Ireland; that Daniel Miller, John Smith, James Foster, and John Huzzey were also born there; and that Michael Dawley, John Dorrance, and Thomas Hughes were of Irish blood if not of Irish birth. Further mention of these will hereinafter be found.

As for such names in the list as Burke, Casey, Connor, Conway, Dailey, Donovan, Doherty, Doyle, Eagan, Fitzgerald, Flanagan, Hackett, Healey, Hagerty, Hogan, and the like, their national character is at once apparent. The same may be said of other names in the list, such as Kelly, Larkin, Maloney, McCarthy, McDermot, McGrath, McNamara, Mullen, Mulligan, Murphy, O'Brian, O'Kelly, O'Neal, Reily, Sullivan, etc.

The Rhode Island Revolutionary rolls also contain

many names that are as much Irish as they are anything else, but which have not been included in the foregoing list for want of definite information concerning their bearers. Thus, for example, we find Blake, Bowen, Carr, Cummings, Dring, Ford, Fox, Halley, Harvey, Hines, Jordan, King, Lee, Stewart, Strange, Vaughan, and so on. Most of these names are to-day found in nearly every populous Irish locality, and doubtless some of those here cited were borne by Rhode Islanders of that blood.

Company clerks and regimental adjutants frequently made unsuccessful attempts at correctly spelling Irish names, as, indeed, they also did with regard to other names. The names were often written merely as they sounded, and as they sometimes sounded differently to different clerks, one result has been, at times, a variety of spelling for the same name.

Much Rhode Island matter relating to the War of Independence has been lost or is so scattered as to be inaccessible. Muster rolls of companies and other documents cannot be found and thus, doubtless, we are deprived of a large number of Irish names which could be added to the roll. These Rhode Islanders of Irish blood must have some descendants living. It would be interesting to know if any of them are comprised in the membership of the patriotic-hereditary societies. A few words now with reference to the individuals, or most of them, in the list here given.

John Dorrance was of a family from Ireland[1] which settled in the present town of Foster, R. I., about 1715–'20. He graduated from Rhode Island College, now Brown

[1] In the *Boston Pilot*, June 29, 1895, is an interesting article on the Rhode Island Dorrances here mentioned.

University, became a member of the General Assembly, a judge, president of the Providence town council for sixteen years, and held many other positions of honor. He died in June, 1813. The Providence *Gazette* in an obituary notice states that "Judge Dorrance was descended from Irish parentage, but was himself born in Foster, this State. He received a degree from Rhode Island College[1] and afterwards became a tutor, and since a member of the corporation of that institution." Continuing, it states that he was of unblemished integrity and undeviating patriotism.

THE ARMY OF OBSERVATION.

Mention is found in the records of George Dorrance and of George Dorrance, Jr. The latter was, in 1775, appointed ensign of the lieutenant-colonel's company of the Regiment of Providence in the "Army of Observation." George Dorrance was, in 1780, appointed lieutenant of the second company of Scituate, R. I. A Capt. George Dorrance appears, in 1781, in a regiment raised by act of the General Assembly. He was doubtless the same individual. In 1782, George Dorrance, Jr., was commissioned major of the Third regiment of militia in the county of Providence. Alex. Dorrance was a member of the company of "Captain General's Cavaliers." His name appears in a pay abstract for service in "the late expedition to Rhode Island"—July 24 to Aug. 31, 1778.

Dr. Henry Sterling, the Irish surgeon already men-

[1] See *The Irish Chapter in the History of Brown University* (*Brown Magazine*, Providence, R. I., March, 1896). Some of the earliest funds for Rhode Island College, now Brown University, were raised in Ireland. Rev. Morgan Edwards went there on a collecting tour. His wife was Mary Nunn, of Cork. See Guild's History of the University.

tioned, settled in Providence in 1756. He died here in 1810. In a notice at the time of his death, the Providence *Gazette* states that Dr. Sterling "was a native of a town in the vicinity of Londonderry, in the Kingdom of Ireland." It also states that he "was in hearty sympathy with the Revolution and aided the patriot cause with his advice and professional services." "Capt. Samuel Allin" is mentioned as "son-in-law of the deceased."

When Washington ordered the advance of two invading divisions into Canada, Rhode Island men were among the first to respond. Captain Simeon Thayer, of Providence, recruited a company, enlisting every man himself. Many Irish served under him at different periods during the war. Among them were: John Barritt, John Carrell, Edward Conner, Thomas Garey, Patrick Hannington, James Hayden, Cornelius Higgarty, or Hagerty, Edward Mulligan, John Ryand (Ryan), Patrick Tracy, and James Welch.

One of the invading divisions was placed under Benedict Arnold, and the other under Richard Montgomery. The latter was an Irishman, a native of Raphoe, in the county Donegal. He had recently been made a brigadier-general. Before Quebec, Montgomery assumed the chief command. Captain Thayer's company had accompanied Arnold's division. Capt. Samuel Ward, of Westerly, R. I., was also in the expedition with his company, which included Thomas Dougherty and John Hickey. Captain Topham, of Newport, R. I., likewise participated with his company, in which were several Irish soldiers.

Another notable participant was Dr. Isaac Senter, of Newport. He was a native of the Londonderry, N. H., Irish settlement. A letter to the writer, a few years ago, from the town clerk of Londonderry states that without much doubt the Senters were from Ireland, as they came to that settlement so soon after the rest. Dr. Senter accompanied the troops to Cambridge as a volunteer surgeon. Later he was appointed a surgeon in the Continental line and assigned to Arnold's division. He was taken prisoner at Quebec but was soon released. Captain Thayer was also captured.

PATRICK TRACY KILLED AT QUEBEC.

The death of the gallant Montgomery prevented the invasion from attaining the results anticipated. Senter, Thayer and others kept journals of the expedition. To these sources we are indebted for many interesting facts. Patrick Tracy, one of Thayer's men, was killed in the assault on Quebec. Cornelius Hagerty and Corporal James Hayden of the same company were wounded. In a work[1] on the period reference is made to John M. Taylor, "keen as an Irish greyhound," who was Arnold's purveyor and commissary in the wilderness. Lieutenant William Cross is described as a "handsome little Irishman, always neatly dressed, and commanded [on the Isle of Orleans] a detachment of about twenty men."

Later, Thayer was commissioned major and was ordered to Rhode Island to support General Sullivan at the siege of Newport. He did not arrive, however, until three days after the battle that ensued. The Major was so great an admirer of General Montgomery, who fell at Quebec, that when, after the war, he established a hotel in Providence he called it the Montgomery hotel. He also named one of his sons Richard Montgomery Thayer, after the distinguished soldier.

[1] Henry.

John McCarthy and Cornelius Sullivan were soldiers of Colonel Elliott's regiment, which was raised in accordance with a recommendation of the "Committee of the New England States" for the defense of Rhode Island. John McCoy, Daniel Lyon, and John Conway also belonged to the regiment. In September, 1776, Captain Hoppin's company numbered in its ranks Edward Murfee and John Driskill. This latter name is now commonly written Driscoll. James Donal was a member of Captain Dyer's company, in Col. Christopher Lippitt's regiment. His name is found in a "Pay abstract" for September, 1776. Correctly, the name may have been O'Donnell or, possibly, McDonnell. Benjamin Burn [Byrne or Burns?] was in September, 1776, of Captain Arnold's company, in Lippitt's regiment.

It is likely that, in some instances, men from other states enlisted in Rhode Island regiments and that men from Rhode Island enlisted in regiments belonging to other states. This, however, does not materially affect our general perspective.

THE GALLANT THOMAS HUGHES.

Thomas Hughes, a gallant Rhode Island soldier, was of Irish descent. He was the only son [1] of Joseph and Mary Hughes and was born May 30, 1752. He was a captain in the Revolution, and a major in the War of 1812. He was a sincere patriot, an accomplished officer and a credit to his Irish ancestry.

[1] I am indebted for the facts here given concerning Thomas Hughes to Miss Mary A. Greene of Providence, R. I., and Mr. Henry L. Greene of Riverpoint, R. I. Miss Greene is descended from Thomas Hughes in her mother's line and from Col. Christopher Greene on her father's side. Mr. Henry L. Greene is a great-grandson of Col. Christopher Greene.

In the Rhode Island Colonial Records he is mentioned as of Freetown, Mass. His name first appears in the Revolutionary Records of Rhode Island in October, 1776, when he is mentioned as second lieutenant in Col. Israel Angell's battalion. In February, 1777, Hughes was chosen to be first lieutenant, and at some time between August and October, 1777, he was raised to the rank of captain. He served with Col. Israel Angell's regiment throughout the war. He was, therefore, present at the brilliant defense of Fort Mercer at Red Bank when the Hessians under Count Donop were repulsed by Captain Hughes's future father-in-law and commanding officer, Col. Christopher Greene. Hughes was with the Rhode Island troops at the battle of Rhode Island, Aug. 29, 1778, and also in May, 1781, when Col. Christopher Greene was murdered by De Lancey's Loyalists in Westchester county, N. Y. Captain Hughes was at that time paymaster.

In 1791 the Rhode Island General Assembly appointed Col. Jeremiah Olney and Capt. Thomas Hughes agents for the proprietors of the Anaquacut farm in Tiverton, R. I., which was set off to the officers and soldiers of the late Continental battalion commanded by Colonel Angell. These agents successfully petitioned the General Assembly to make up a considerable deficiency demanded of them by the purchasers to whom they sold the land, and a resurvey was consequently ordered.

Thomas Hughes was one of the original members of the Rhode Island Society of the Cincinnati, and appears on that society's record thus: "Capt. Thomas Hughes 1st R. I. Continental Infantry." His Revolutionary record, as compiled by Heitman, in his volume, *Officers of the Continental Army*, is as follows:

"Hughes, Thomas, (R. I.) 2nd Lieutenant 11th Continental Infantry 1st January to 31st December, 1776; 1st Lieutenant 2nd Rhode Island, 1st January 1777; Captain, 23rd June 1777; transferred to 1st Rhode Island 1st January 1781, and served to close of war."

Thomas Hughes also served throughout the War of 1812, with the rank of major, and his widow drew a pension till her death in 1844. He died Dec. 10, 1821, at his home at Centreville, R. I., in the northwestern part of the town of Warwick, R. I., and was buried in a family burying ground near by and later transferred. In April, 1896, his second burial place was abandoned and the bodies were removed to Greenwood cemetery, Phenix, R. I., including the remains of Major Hughes, his wife and maiden daughter Sally. A marker of the Sons of the American Revolution has been placed at his grave, his being among the first fifty names drawn by lot by the Rhode Island Society of the Sons of the American Revolution.

THE CHILDREN OF THOMAS HUGHES.

Thomas Hughes married Feb. 27, 1782, Welthian (born Nov. 19, 1757; died, 1844), eldest child of Col. Christopher and Anne (Lippitt) Greene of Centreville, Warwick, R. I. The children of Thomas and Welthian Hughes were:

1. Mary, born Jan. 4, 1783, married Burrows Aborn, and had eight children, all of whom died unmarried.

2. Christopher Greene, born July 9, 1785; died at New Orleans, La., July 22, 1815, unmarried. (A sea captain.)

3. Phebe, born Sept. 1, 1787, married her mother's first cousin, Jeremiah, son of (Judge) William and

Welthian (Lippitt) Greene of Occupasnetuxet, Warwick, R. I. Her issue, viz., three grandchildren and two great-grandchildren, are the only living descendants of Thomas Hughes.

4. Katy, born Aug. 16, 1789, died in infancy.
5. Sally, born Dec. 15, 1790; died unmarried (1845).
6. Elizabeth, born Feb. 2, 1792; died in infancy.
7. John Luther, born Nov. 2, 1795; died Jan. 14, 1863.

The latter was a prominent merchant and manufacturer in Rhode Island, and as a member of the common council of the city of Providence was actively instrumental in devising, framing and establishing the public school system of the city. He was the first secretary of the Rhode Island Mutual Fire Insurance Company. He had a refined literary taste, inherited from both his parents, and a large public spirit. He married Eliza, daughter of (Col.) Jeremiah and Anne (Keene) Whiting, and had several children, all of whom died young.

Thomas Hughes, the subject of this sketch, was a man of great energy and much executive ability, and had a fondness for good literature.

SEVENTEEN SOLDIERS OF LIBERTY.

Mention of the following seventeen soldiers who served in Rhode Island commands, during the Revolution, is found in a report of the secretary of war (1835), relative to the pension establishment of the United States:

David Kelly, a private in the Rhode Island Continental line. He was still living in 1834, in which year he was placed on the pension roll.

Jeremiah Whelan, a private in the Rhode Island line; placed on the pension roll in 1819.

Stephen Long, a private in the Rhode Island line; placed on the pension roll in 1818.

Philip Griffin of the Rhode Island line. He died May 9, 1832.

Daniel Dawley, a private in the "Rhode Island Militia"; placed on the pension roll. He died in 1832.

Thomas Powers, of the Rhode Island line; placed on the pension roll in 1818.

Malachi Green, a private in the "Rhode Island Militia"; placed on the pension roll in 1834.

Stephen Kelly, placed on the pension roll in 1833; a private in the Rhode Island militia.

Martin Murphy, a private in the Rhode Island militia; placed on the pension roll in 1833.

John Welsh, 2d, a sergeant in the Rhode Island line; placed on the pension roll in 1821.

Matthew Hanley, of Angell's regiment; died May 26, 1804. This may have been the soldier who is elsewhere mentioned as Matthew Hendly.

Martin Herrick, of the Rhode Island line; placed on the pension roll in 1819.

Thomas Gleeson, of the Rhode Island line; died Aug. 5, 1833.

John Larkin, a private in the Rhode Island militia; placed on the pension roll in 1833.

Matthew Bennett, of the Rhode Island line; placed on the pension roll in 1819.

Joseph Bennett, of the "Rhode Island state troops and militia"; placed on the pension roll in 1833.

James Bennett, of the Rhode Island line; placed on the pension roll in 1833.

OTHER NAMES IN THE RECORDS.

Mention is also found in official records of the Revolution of Jeremiah Martin, of Providence county. He is credited with service in the Rhode Island militia. He was still living in 1831. Joseph Carroll, another pensioner, was living in 1833. He is described as of Kent county, and is credited with services in the militia. Thomas Long, described as of Providence county, was a mariner and served in the Continental navy. He died in 1821.

The Irish name Moore was borne by a number of Rhode Islanders in the Revolution. Christopher Moore was a private in Col. Lippitt's regiment. Later, a Christopher Moore belonged to Capt. Humphries company of Col. Angell's regiment. John Moore was of Capt. Carr's company in Col. Richmond's regiment. In 1776, William Moore and Thomas Ray are mentioned as of Col. Elliott's regiment.

The records likewise speak of Thomas Carey, a "recruit from Tiverton," 1782; of John Cowen, an ensign, as early as 1776, in Col. Lippitt's regiment; of Sergt. Peter Cowen who was of Col. Archibald Crary's regiment, and of Stephen Cowen who was in Capt. Hoppin's company of Lippitt's command. William Ennis became a sergeant and is mentioned as of Col. Sherburn's command.

The rolls of Col. Topham's regiment include the names Lieut. Daniel Wall, Corp. Thomas Reynolds, James Reynolds, Stephen Rany, James Knox, and Richard Hayden. The rolls of Col. Israel Angell's regiment include the names Joseph Manning, Benjamin Jackson and others herein mentioned. John Conley of Providence, was, in 1777, mentioned as enlisted in Capt. Lewis' company in the Continental service. It is likely that some men after their term of enlistment had expired, reënlisted into other regiments, as we frequently find the same name in different commands. In some cases, of course, it may have been borne by different individuals.

William Parker, John Wilson, and James Bishop, of the list [1] here given, were, as has been stated, natives of Ireland. In 1775 they were members of Captain Topham's company, of Col. Thomas Church's regiment, which was recruited in Newport and Bristol counties, Rhode Island.

Parker was born in County Waterford, Ireland, and at the time of his enlistment was about forty-one years of age. He is described in a return as a laborer, and as having brown hair and brown eyes. His height was five feet, four and one half inches.

Wilson was born in County Kilkenny, Ireland. He was a trunk maker. His age is given in the return as twenty-two years.

Bishop was a native of Dublin, a carpenter by trade, and was aged twenty-six years. He had dark hair and blue eyes.

Dennis Hogan, Tobias Burk, William Crou, and Philip Doolinty—all Irishmen—were likewise members of Captain Topham's company in Church's regiment. Hogan was a native of Limerick, Ireland. He was by trade a "limner." In a return his age is given as twenty-four years. He had black hair and gray eyes. In the return mentioned his name is incorrectly spelled "Hogain." He was probably the Sergt. Dennis Hogan of whom

[1] See roll of Capt. John Topham's company, as published in the New England Historical and Genealogical Register.

mention is frequently made. Burk was also a native of Limerick, Ireland. He was a weaver, had light hair and blue eyes, and in 1775 was about twenty years of age. In a return his first name is given as "Tobiat." Correctly, this was doubtless Tobias. Crou was a native of County Waterford, Ireland, twenty years of age, a mariner, and had light hair and blue eyes. The name Crou is an odd one. The correct form may have been Crowe or Carew. Philip Doolinty is mentioned as a native of "Tamonas Town, Kileaney," which was probably the company clerk's best attempt at writing Thomastown, Kilkenny.[1] Philip was a laborer, had brown hair and blue eyes and, in 1775, was aged twenty-two years.

A SOLDIER OF CAPTAIN FIELD'S COMPANY.

Manie O'Daniel was a soldier of Capt. John Field's company in Colonel Hitchcock's regiment. He is later mentioned as of Capt. Simeon Thayer's company as the latter was made up from different commands near Boston for the expedition to Canada under Benedict Arnold. This odd name—Manie—is a form of Manus. James Hayden, as mentioned elsewhere, was a corporal in this company of Thayer's.

David Healy (also spelled Healey) served, in 1776, in

[1] Kilkenny—a county from which have come a number of prominent Rhode Islanders. George Berkeley, the brilliant Irishman who arrived at Newport, R. I., in 1729, was a native of the county, and was known as "the Kilkenny scholar." Stephen Jackson, a native of Kilkenny, was born in the year 1700, and came to this country about 1724. In 1745 he was a resident of Providence, R. I., where he is mentioned as a "schoolmaster." One of his descendants, Charles Jackson, became governor of Rhode Island. Rev. James Wilson, who for many years was pastor of the "Round Top" church in Providence, R. I., is also stated to have been from Kilkenny. Hon. Thomas Davis, who was elected to Congress from Rhode Island in 1853, was a Kilkenny man, and so was the late Roman Catholic Bishop Hendricken of Providence.

Capt. Loring Peck's company of Colonel Lippitt's regiment. John Mitchell was in Capt. Benjamin Hoppin's company of the same regiment. Edward Murfee, Philip Morris, and John Driskill also served in Captain Hoppin's company of Lippitt's regiment. Joseph Burke was of Capt. John Whipple's company "doing duty on Rhode Island," March, 1781.

Stephen Daily, Edward Morris, Joseph Norton, Robert Kennady, and Joseph Gaffery saw service in Col. John Topham's regiment. Solomon Dailey was of the fourth company of Colonel Hitchcock's regiment of the army of observation.

John Conway, John McCloud, Anthony Murray, Thomas Hart, and John McCoy served with fidelity in Col. Robert Elliott's regiment. Lawrence McLouth, Barney Clarke, John Lawless, and William Lawless belonged to Col. Archibald Crary's regiment. William Lawless became a captain, Edward Bennett was of Capt. Jeremiah Olney's company, Hitchcock's regiment, 1775.

William McCoy was quartermaster sergeant in Capt. Thomas Cole's company in Col. Christopher Greene's command. James Daily was in the same company. Peter Daily is mentioned as of Capt. E. Lewis' company, in Col. Christopher Greene's regiment, in 1779-'80. The following mention is made of this company on one occasion:

Newport, 6th Jan'y, 1780. Mustered then the 3[d] Company as specified in the above Roll.

     DANL. S. DEXTER,
      Commiss. of Muster, Pro tem.

Andrew Boyd, who is stated to have been of Irish extraction, was a charter member, 1774, of the Kentish Guards of East Greenwich, R. I. On the morning after the battle of Lexington, the Guards, numbering 110 men, rank and file, left East Greenwich on the march for the scene of action. They had proceeded as far as Pawtucket, R. I., when they received an express informing them of the result of the battle. They, thereupon, returned to East Greenwich, but continued on duty, there.

The Boyds were a numerous family in East Greenwich, R. I., and vicinity. Some of them were born in Ireland; all are believed to have been of Irish blood. The given name Andrew frequently occurs in the family. One Andrew Boyd of Rhode Island is mentioned as a native of the County Antrim, Ireland, of which place his mother, Sarah (Moore) Boyd, was also a native. Another Andrew, probably the one mentioned in the charter of the Kentish Guards, is thus referred to in the records of the General Assembly, October, 1776: "In council was read the return of Andrew Boyd, clerk of the company of Kentish Guards, choosing Christopher Greene, of Warwick, son of Nathaniel, second lieutenant of said company, in the room of Thomas Holden, who refused."

Edward Casey served in Col. Archibald Crary's regiment. Oliver Kelly and Duncan Kelly are mentioned as Barrington, R. I., soldiers who served under Capt. Thomas Allin. Corporal William Kelley was of the Barrington militia guard in 1778.

Among the residents of Warren, R. I., in May, 1778, when the town was raided and pillaged by the enemy was the Rev. Erasmus Kelley. He had gone to Warren from Newport when the latter place was taken possession of by the British under Pigot. During the raid on Warren, Rev. Mr. Kelley lost nearly all his household effects, which were taken or destroyed by the foe. Many other residents of Warren suffered in like manner.

JOHN O'KELLEY OF CAPTAIN ORMSBEE'S COMPANY.

John O'Kelley was in 1776 a member of Capt. Ezra Ormsbee's company[1] of militia in the town of Warren, R. I. Among others in the company were Daniel Kelley and Joseph Kelley. The General Assembly, in 1782, gave " Mrs. Elizabeth O'Kelley of Warren, widow and administratrix of John O'Kelley," permission to sell certain real estate. In 1794, a Kelly was empowered by the General Assembly " to erect a toll bridge over Kelly's ferry in Warren."

Joseph McMilon was a member of Capt. Ezra Ormsbee's company, of Warren, in 1776, while among the Warren soldiers in 1777 were Joseph McMillion (probably another form of the name) and Peter McMillion. This name McMillion may have been McMillen, McMallon, or McMullen—all three of which are found in Ireland. In a deed dated June 1, 1798, Peter McMillan and his wife, Sarah, are shown to have been at that date residents of Galway, Saratoga county, New York.

Peter McMillen was of the crew of the privateer *General Stark* of Warren. Whether he was the soldier mentioned as Peter McMillion the writer is unable to state. The *General Stark* was of some 130 tons burden and carried fourteen guns. William O'Brien and John Killey were members of Capt. Curtis Cole's company, 1781, in Col.

[1] Miss Virginia Baker's *History of Warren, Rhode Island, in the War of the Revolution*. (Warren, R. I., 1901.)

Nathan Miller's regiment. O'Brien and Killey were both probably of Warren.[1] The former sometimes appears as O'Briant and O'Brient.

BRIEF MENTION OF EIGHTEEN IRISHMEN.

Michael Wright was a native of Mountmellick, Queen's county, Ireland. He is described as a ribbon weaver. He enlisted at Providence, January, 1781, and served in a Rhode Island regiment of the line. He may have also served in other organizations in campaigns previous to 1781. He is mentioned in a return as 42 years of age and as having his residence in "Seacunnet," R. I. His enlistment here mentioned was for three years.

Mark Barns who also served in the Rhode Island Continentals was born in Waterford, Ireland, and at the time of his enlistment resided in Providence, R. I. His age is given as 28 years. He was by trade a "wine cooper." He enlisted "for the war" and is described as having brown hair and a "fresh complexion."

James Foster was a native of Dublin, Ireland. He enlisted at Coventry, R. I., was 47 years of age, had

---

[1] The town of Warren, R. I., was named in honor of an Irishman, Sir Peter Warren. Several pages in O'Hart's *Irish Pedigrees* are devoted to the Warrens of Ireland. A copy of the work can be found in the Providence Public Library. Edward Warren served the Stuart cause in Ireland and at one time had command of the citadel of Belfast. After the fall of Limerick he went to France. A Patrick Warren is mentioned in 1559. Capt. Edward Warren was among the Confederated Catholics, at Kilkenny, in 1646. In 1689, Capt. John Warren was a member of the Irish parliament. Anthony Warren, a son of Sir William Warren, married the widow of Sir Cahir O' Dougherty, Knt. Col. Henry Warren was among the Catholic defenders of Drogheda during the siege of the latter, in 1649, by Cromwell. The Irish Warrens became so prominent that Warrenstown, in the County Meath, was named after them. Bearers of the name were also found in Dublin, Carlow, Queen's, Kildare and other Irish counties. Some of the Clan O'Byrne took the name Warren. In 1774, a Captain Warren was with the Irish brigade in France and held a commission in the Regiment of Dillon. A Lieutenant Warren served in the Irish Legion organized by Napoleon Bonaparte.

"gray hair" and a "fresh complexion." The date of his enlistment is given as January, 1781, and was "for the war." Like others, he may have been a veteran of previous campaigns.

James Hayes was born in Cork, Ireland. He is described in the roll as 25 years of age, and a "mariner." He enlisted at Bristol, R. I., January, 1781, for three years.

Cornelius Driskill was a native of Kinsale, County Cork, Ireland. He became a resident of Providence, R. I., and is referred to as a "mariner." He is mentioned in the roll as 18 years of age. He enlisted into the Rhode Island Continental line, in January, 1781, "for three years."

James King was born in Dublin, Ireland, and resided in Providence, R. I. He was a tailor by trade, had black hair and a light complexion, and enlisted at Providence "for the war." The regimental rolls mention him as 25 years of age.

John Huzzey was a native of Armagh, Ireland. He enlisted in January, 1777, "for the war." His age is given as 50 years. He had gray hair and a light complexion.

Matthew Hendly was born in Limerick, Ireland. He was a barber by trade. His age is given on the regimental rolls as 30 years.

Michael Killey [correctly, probably Kelley] was a native of Limerick, Ireland. He was a barber, 5 ft. 6 in. in height and had dark hair and a dark complexion. He resided in Newport, R. I. His age is given in a return as 36 years.

Daniel Monks was a native of Ireland, a barber by trade and resided at Newport, R. I. He enlisted at Newport "for the war." His age is given as 64 years. He is mentioned as a private in Capt. Thomas Hughes' company, of Angell's command, and also as serving under Olney and in " Col. Greene's Regiment of Foot."

Daniel Miller was a weaver. He was born in Ireland, had light hair and a light complexion and enlisted at Providence, R. I., Jan. 1, 1777, "for the war." He is mentioned as 30 years of age.

Charles Watson, a weaver, was born in Ireland. He enlisted Jan. 1, 1777, "for the war." He appears on the rolls as 25 years of age.

Peter Burns, another Irishman, enlisted at North Kingstown, R. I., in January, 1777, "for the war." He was 43 years of age.

Michael Doharty [also spelled Doherty] was a native of Donegal, Ireland, and enlisted at Providence, R. I., in April, 1777, "for the war." He was a young man, 22 years of age.

Edward Fitzgerald of Newport, R. I., was born in Tipperary, Ireland, and is mentioned as of the Rhode Island Continentals when he was 19 years of age. He is spoken of elsewhere herein.

Peter Morrison, who is mentioned as from "Ireland," served in Col. Israel Angell's regiment.

James Madden, from "Ireland," likewise served in Angell's regiment.

John Mahony, from "Ireland," is mentioned as of the second battalion of Angell's regiment.

OTHER NAMES IN THE RHODE ISLAND RECORDS.

Timothy Mahony is spoken of as serving under Captain Sprague in 1777.

Patrick McMullan is mentioned in the Rhode Island records as a marine aboard the sloop *Providence*, Continental navy. He entered Jan. 5, 1776.

Patrick McNamara was a marine aboard the ship *Alfred*, Continental navy. The Rhode Island records mention him.

John McLaughlin was a marine and served on the *Columbus* of the Continental navy.

Hugh McCowan was also a marine and served on the *Columbus*. He is mentioned as early as 1776.

Matthew McCaffray was a marine aboard the sloop *Providence*, Continental navy. He entered in 1776. The Rhode Island records state that he was "Left sick at Providence, fever."

Dennis McCartel is mentioned as a private in 1776 and is also referred to as having had "previous service."

Patrick Harrington was a private in Capt. Simeon Thayer's company and went with Thayer in the expedition to Canada and was taken prisoner at Quebec. He may have been the soldier mentioned elsewhere as Patrick Hannington.

Hugh Kenady was a soldier credited to West Greenwich, R. I. The name is also found spelled Kinady, Kennady, etc. Peter Cowen was a sergeant in Col. Archibald Crary's regiment. Barnabus Hicks served under Col. William Richmond.

John Sullivan and William Sullivan, both of Rhode Island, are mentioned in the Massachusetts records as serving on the ship *Deane*. John's age is given as 16 years, and William, aged 25 years, is mentioned as a "volunteer" on the ship. The *Deane* was commanded by Elisha Hinman.

WILLIAM MC COY OF GREENE'S REGIMENT.

The records also mention a William McCoy. He was quartermaster sergeant in Capt. Thomas Cole's company of Col. Christopher Greene's regiment. John Murray[1] and Samuel Dunn[2] were members of "the Providence Company of Cadets," under Colonel Nightingale, stationed at Pawtuxet, R. I., from Jan. 7 to Feb. 7, 1777. A participant named Dunn is mentioned in connection with the *Gaspee* affair. In one place his given name is stated to have been Benjamin. Another authority, however, inclines to the belief that it was Samuel.

John Welch, at first an ensign in Captain Hoxsie's

[1] The Irish Murrays trace descent from a remote period, and have produced many people of distinction. The name derives from O'Muireadhaigh ("Muir," Irish : the sea ; and "eadhach" or "eadhaigh," a protector or garment). The Irish form has been anglicized O'Murray, Murray, Murry, etc. The prefixes Mac and Kil are also found in Ireland in connection with the name, *i. e.*, MacMurray and Kilmurray. A Clan O'Murray was at one period in Irish history prominent in the territory of Brefney, which included the modern counties of Cavan and Leitrim and parts of Meath and Sligo. Also prominent in Brefney were the clans O'Rourke, O'Reilly, O'Carroll, O'Fay, MacDonnell, MacHugh, MacManus, MacCogan and others of note. O'Murrays were also chieftains of Ceara, in Mayo, and of the Lagan, in Mayo. The name Murray at present abounds throughout Ireland. Whether the Murrays of Scotland are kin to the Murrays of Ireland is a topic often discussed. It is possible that both had a common Gaelic origin going back to the days when Ireland (Scotia Major) was the mother country of Scotland (Scotia Minor).

[2] Dunn, a typical Irish name; from the Irish O'Duin, anglicized O'Dunn, Dunn, Dunne, Dun, and Doyne. Some of the Irish Dunns may have derived their name from *dun*—a fort—illustrated in the Irish names Dun-luce, Dun-more, Dun-manway etc.

company, of a Rhode Island regiment, became a lieutenant in Colonel Topham's command, and was later attached to Col. Jeremiah Olney's regiment. He received a staff appointment as quartermaster.

It is a well-known fact that a project was undertaken during the Revolution to raise a regiment of Rhode Island slaves. Those enlisting were thereby to be made free, and their former masters were to be compensated by the state. James Burk of Providence had a slave who thus enlisted. He was named Africa Burk, and his master valued him at £120.

The General Assembly in March, 1781, refers to the farm in Exeter, R. I., "lately belonging to Samuel Boone," leased to Michael Dawley by the state for £91. This was one of the Irish Dawleys, a family that became quite numerous in Rhode Island. Many of its descendants are still found in the state. Boone, just mentioned, was a loyalist, and his farm had been confiscated. It was provided by the General Assembly that Dawley should pay the rental in produce for the troops. Michael Dawley is mentioned[1] as belonging to a militia company during the Revolution. He was still living in 1834.

John Herrington (or Harrington) was made an ensign in Capt. Stephen Sheldon's company, in November, 1776. The company formed part of Colonel Sayles' regiment. Maj. John Clark[2] who, for quite a period during the Revolution was an aide to Gen. Nathaniel Greene, was the grandson of an Irish weaver. On one occasion, having captured a British standard, he was

---

[1] In a report of the secretary of war relative to the pension establishment of the United States (Washington, D. C., 1835).
[2] Not known to be a Rhode Islander.

offered £200 to return it, but rejected the proposal with scorn.

EDWARD BURKE, LIEUTENANT OF MARINES.

Edward Burke was a lieutenant of marines, and served on the ship *Columbus*, Continental navy. He entered Dec. 29, 1776. Was discharged at Newport, R. I., Oct. 19, 1777.

Timothy Burke served in Capt. James Parker's company, of Col. Christopher Smith's regiment. He enlisted February, 1777, for fifteen months.

George O'Harra was "armorer's mate" on the ship *Alfred*, Continental navy, 1776.

Peter Morris was a marine, and served on the ship *Columbus*, Continental navy. He was discharged at Newport, R. I.

Joseph Moran served in Capt. Robert Carr's company, of Col. Nathan Miller's regiment of militia. Moran is supposed to have belonged in Warren, R. I., or vicinity. A Joseph Moran is mentioned as of Barrington, R. I. He may have been the same.

Elizabeth Obrian [O'Brian] was a nurse in a hospital during the Revolution. She is mentioned in a pay abstract covering the period from Jan. 1, 1778, to Nov. 1, 1778.

John M. O'Brien was a Rhode Island Continental soldier. He served in Capt. J. Dexter's company, of the "Late Col. Greene's regiment." He enlisted on Feb. 1, 1781, for a term of three years, and died on Nov. 19, 1781. He was doubtless the soldier who is elsewhere mentioned in the Rhode Island records as John Morris O'Brien.

Patrick O'Brian was a marine, and served aboard the *Alfred*, being later transferred to the *Columbus*.

William O'Brient [O'Brien] is mentioned as of Sergt Nathan Barden's company, town guard at Warren, R. I. The name William O'Bryan, probably the same individual, is found in a military account book, 1778, Warren, R. I.

William O'Brient [O'Brien] served in Colonel Angell's Rhode Island regiment of Continentals, having enlisted "for the war." Whether he was the William O'Brient referred to as of Warren, R. I., is not known.

Charles Kelly is believed to have been of Richmond, R. I. He was taken prisoner at Fort Washington, and is referred to as "a prisoner upon parole."

Richard Harrington was "drafted by Jonathan Mattison from alarum companies" in the town of Coventry, R. I., 1778.

Thomas Kelley was a "tender, general hospital," 1778-'79.

William Kelley, elsewhere referred to herein, was a corporal in Sergt. Josiah Humphry's guard of militia stationed at Barrington, R. I., 1778.

TIMOTHY KELLY OF CAPTAIN WEST'S COMPANY.

Timothy Kelly served as a private in Capt. Benjamin West's company, 1777.

Thomas Cary was a sergeant in Captain Fenner's company, of Colonel Lippitt's regiment, 1776-'77. A

Thomas Carey, perhaps the same, was a sergeant in Capt. Joseph Sprague's company, of Colonel Brown's regiment, Rhode Island militia, in 1779.

William Cary appears as a private in Capt. William Lawless' company, of Colonel Crary's regiment.

Bernard Galligher served on the sloop *Providence*, Continental navy. Entered Sept. 4, 1776. Taken from the *Favourite*.

Philip Driskel, Jr., served in 1776, in Captain Joseph Pendleton's company of militia, Westerly, R. I.

Richard Driskill was a matross in Colonel Elliott's regiment of artillery, 1779.

Michael Moore is mentioned as a private of marines on the ship *Alfred*.

John Riley was a matross in Colonel Elliott's artillery regiment. He enlisted July 17, 1779.

Daniel Jackson is mentioned in a return, 1777, as major of the Independent Company of Light Infantry, Providence county, R. I.

John Joyce belonged to a militia company of Warwick, R. I. He is credited with service in 1777.

Patrick Hickey served in Angell's regiment. In one place he is reported as sick at Warren, R. I.

Patten Fitzgerald of Providence enlisted here June 22, 1780, and served in the Continental line.

David Burk is mentioned as of Capt. James Parker's company, in Col. Christopher Smith's regiment. He was enlisted by Captain Parker April 3, 1777, for fifteen months.

John Burk, from "Ireland," served in the second battalion of Colonel Angell's command.

Matthew Bryan served under Captain Dexter during the war.

James Bryan is mentioned as "In 6th Company, signs receipt to Daniel S. Dexter, Py'mr, Dated May 28, 1781." A James Bryan is also mentioned as "Musick," 5th Company in R. I. Regiment of Foot, July, 1782.

MICHAEL KELLEY OF COLONEL GREENE'S REGIMENT.

Michael Kelley is mentioned in a return of Colonel Greene's Regiment of Foot, March 22, 1781, as "on command on the lines."

Eleazar Kelley was a corporal at one period in Colonel Crary's regiment.

James M'Case, was born in Ireland, and resided at Newport, R. I. He was a private in the "Ninth Regiment of Foot, U. S. service, Col. Crary commanding."

Stephen Killey was a private in "Col. Fry's regiment at Warren," R. I., 1777.

Gerrald Fitzgerrald [Gerald Fitzgerald] was a "Quarter-Gunner" aboard the ship *Columbus*. He entered Jan. 7, 1776. He was discharged at Newport.

John Griffin is mentioned as of an "Invalid regiment." His name appears in a "copy of order for payment of wages, etc., allowed for services while in I [Invalid] regiment. Dated Constitution Island, June 15, 1783."

James Griffen was a private in Captain Springer's company, of Colonel Topham's regiment. In one place he is mentioned as "Sick in Gen. Cornell's hospital at Tiverton," R. I., 1779.

William Driskill was of Capt. Joseph Pendleton's militia company, of Westerly, R. I., 1776.

Joseph Forde served as a private in Lieutenant-Colonel Smith's regiment. He was enlisted by Lieut. Henry Alexander, of Captain Parker's company, Dec. 23, 1776.

Daniel Sullivan was a private in Captain Whipple's company, in Col. Christopher Olney's regiment.

David Dowd served in the second company of Warwick, R. I., under Squire Millerd, captain.

Thomas Burns was surgeon's mate aboard the ship *Columbus*. He entered Jan. 18, 1776.

William Burns was a seaman on the *Alfred*. He "shipped at Rhode Island," Dec. 29, 1775.

John M'Clanen, from " Ireland " served in the second battalion of Colonel Angell's command.

John McGowan was rated as a landsman aboard the ship *Columbus*. He entered Jan. 4, 1776.

Charles McDonald served as a seaman on the *Columbus*.

The Rhode Island records also mention a native of Ireland named Johnston—first name not given—who was a resident of Bristol, R. I., and served in the " Ninth Regiment of Foot, U. S. service," under Colonel Crary.

Edward Bennett was of Colonel Hitchcock's regiment. He is mentioned as having sustained the " loss of left arm above elbow in action with enemy at Harlem Heights, on Fort Island, Sept. 10, 1776."

OTHER MENTION IN THE RECORDS.

Peter Nagle, who came from " Ireland," served in Colonel Angell's regiment. Peter Nagel, doubtless the same, is credited with service in Capt. Stephen Olney's company of the regiment. He enlisted March 18, 1777.

Arthur Nagle was a marine on the ship *Columbus*, Continental navy.

James Casey served as a private in the company of Capt. Billings Throope. Mention is made of him in the records of Rhode Island.

Thomas Murray, a marine, served on the *Columbus*. He entered Dec. 18, 1775.

Joseph Murrey was a private in Colonel Elliott's regiment.

Patrick Capron served in Col. Angell's regiment of Continentals. So did Edward Murfey who is recorded as from "Ireland." In 1777, Murfey (also spelled Murfy), was of Capt. Stephen Olney's company in the regiment.

All the commanders of Rhode Island regiments from the opening until the close of hostilities—Church, Topham, Elliott, Crary, Sayles, Angell, Sherburn, Olney, Greene, and the rest—had, no doubt, many Irish at all times in their respective commands.

Samuel Black is believed to have been related to Alexander and James Black, Irish merchants of Providence. In 1776 he was ensign in Capt. Asa Kimball's company of Colonel Sayles' regiment. In 1779 he was lieutenant in Capt. David Howell's company of Providence, and in 1781 was lieutenant in Capt. Benjamin Hoppin's artillery company of Providence.

Patrick Foy and James Lowery, of the list here presented, were from Hopkinton, R. I., and enlisted in Colonel Smith's regiment, the former in 1777 and the latter the year previous. Lawrence McLouth and Anthony Murray are names found on the muster rolls of Col. Archibald

Crary's regiment. And so the subject grows in interest as we proceed.

In July, 1778, "A return of the soldiers enlisted for the town of North Kingstown" included Patrick Duyer (possibly Dwyer), John Duyer, William Harvey, John Kennedy, and John Hogen.

In March, 1780, there was made "A return of all the matrosses in Colonel Robert Elliott's regiment of artillery." The return contains such names as McCarty, Morris, Murray, and McCoy. In another place appears the enlistment into the same regiment of Cornelius Sullivan, already mentioned. Luke Doyle also joined the same regiment, and among others in the command were John Barry, Patt Dunphy, William Fee, Charles Mullen, Thomas Conner, Michael Dorothy (probably Doherty), Edward Donnelly, and Matthew Barr. From which it is evident there was plenty of Irish blood in the command.

Ensign M. Carthy (doubtless intended for Ensign McCarthy) appears in "A weekly return of the Second Battalion of Foot, raising for the state of Rhode Island, and commanded by Colonel Israel Angell." John Tracy, mentioned in the list, was an aide-de-camp on the staff of General Glover at the operations on the island of Rhode Island under Gen. John Sullivan. The appointment was announced Aug. 15, 1778. William M'Carty also served in Sullivan's forces at that period. M'Carty took part in the siege of Newport and the battle that ensued.

"THE BEST FOUGHT ACTION OF THE WAR."

This engagement was pronounced by Lafayette to be " the best fought action of the war," and the Congress tendered Sullivan, son of the Irish schoolmaster, and his officers and men its warm thanks for their fortitude and bravery displayed in the action of August 29, in which they repulsed the British forces and maintained the field. Sullivan was also complimented by the states of Rhode Island and New Hampshire. In addition to two of his brothers—James and Eben—there also served under Sullivan in that engagement Lieutenant-Colonel Hackett, Edward Phelon, and other officers of Irish lineage.

On his retirement from the command of the Rhode Island department in 1779, General Sullivan was presented a number of addresses. He was entertained at a banquet in Providence, and on leaving town was accompanied some distance by Generals Glover and Varnum, officers from each corps of the army, and many leading citizens. An artillery salute of thirteen guns rounded out the farewell.

William M'Carty, just alluded to, upon returning with Sullivan's forces to Providence from the island of Rhode Island, is mentioned,[1] together with Captain Hodgkins and Lieutenant Pierce, as having taken up quarters at the house of Captain Frazer's wife, whose husband was then at sea.

Patrick McKown was a wagoner attached to the quartermaster-general's department at Providence.

Alfred Joyce, a native of Warwick, R. I., enlisted into a Massachusetts regiment at West Point. He enlisted April 13, 1779, and had perhaps seen previous service. His first name is sometimes rendered as Alford.

William Lawless was made a captain under Colonel Crary in 1778. A year later he was "captain-lieutenant" of the colonel's company in the first battalion of infantry. Edward Ross was an ensign in the Second Infantry company of Westerly. William Creed became a captain. It

[1] New England Historical and Genealogical Register, Vol. VII, page 138. (Footnote.)

is a matter of record that the deputy-governor once lent him " twenty-five three-pound shot, a ladle and worm."

Terence Reily's name appears in a return made in 1780. He was probably the schoolmaster of the name resident in Providence, of whom mention [1] is elsewhere found.

James Flanagan and Edward Fitzgerald, elsewhere referred to, are mentioned in the " Muster and Size Rolls of Recruits Enlisted for the Town of Newport for the Campaign of 1782." Flanagan and Fitzgerald were at one time stationed at Ticonderoga. They were enlisted for nine months, though both had seen service in previous campaigns.

In Colonel Topham's command, 1776, are found John Casey, Benjamin Hackett, Joseph Gaffery, Stephen Daily, James Read, Robert Kennedy, Edward Morris and Charles McMillen.

In Colonel Crary's regiment were included Lawrence Clarke, Edward Casey, William McCoy, Eseck Kelly, John Lawless, and others whose names are indicative of Irish lineage.

Joseph Read, James Martin, David Healey, Peter McMillion and Edward Murfee were, at one time, members of Colonel Lippitt's regiment.

Corp. Daniel Hayden and Michael Cooney were, in 1779, of Captain Allen's company, in Angell's regiment. Cooney is mentioned in a " List of Officers and Men who have died in, or been honorably discharged from, Colonel Angell's regiment." James Butler of Cumberland and

---

[1] *Irish Schoolmasters in the American Colonies, 1640-1775, with a Continuation of the Subject During and after the War of the Revolution.* (Washington, D. C., 1898.) *Early Irish Educators of American Youth.* (The *Monitor*, San Francisco, Cal., Oct., 1902.)

Bartholomew Jackson of Newport were in the service in 1782.

PROUD OF THEIR IRISH ANCESTRY.

The grotesque "Scotch-Irish" phantasm has never found a congenial atmosphere in Rhode Island. Descendants here of Irish Revolutionary stock take an especial pride in being connected with a race, which, as President Andrew Jackson said in an address to the Boston Charitable Irish Society, "has so much to recommend it to the good wishes of the world."[1] There are old Rhode Islanders who value their Irish line of descent very highly indeed.

In 1777 mention is made in the records of the General Assembly of Timothy Larkin, "a sick soldier on duty in this state." The Rhode Island Larkins were of Irish blood, people of the name settling here in early colonial days. Some of their descendants are still living in the state. Edward Larkin, a Rhode Island settler, is heard from at Newport as early as 1655. His name appears in the "Roule of ye Freemen of ye colonie of everie Towne." Larkin, or O'Larkin, is a well-known Irish name. The clan's territory in Ireland was known as the "O'Larkin's Country." John Larkin was a member for Hopkinton, R. I., of the "committee to procure arms and accoutrements," 1776.

[1] This address by President Jackson was delivered in Boston, June 22, 1833, in reply to one on behalf of the Society. The Society called upon him during his stay at the Tremont House, that city, and these addresses resulted. In the course of his remarks, Jackson said: "It is with great pleasure that I see so many of the countrymen of my father assembled on this occasion. I have always been proud of my ancestry and of being descended from that noble race, and rejoice that I am so nearly allied to a country which has so much to recommend it to the good wishes of the world." The Charitable Irish Society which was founded in 1737 is still in existence. Jackson was a member of the Hibernian Society of Philadelphia, his membership certificate bearing date of March 23, 1819.

Patrick Caton was in Colonel Angell's Continental regiment, already mentioned, as were also John Ragen and Dennis Bagley,—all three of Providence. There likewise served in Angell's command: John Tuley, Michael Stafford, Joseph Manning, Thomas Mitchell, and James Patrick. The latter surname may have correctly been Gilpatrick or Fitzpatrick. Richard Shield and John Gibbon, soldiers of the Revolution, appear as enlisted from Newport.

In March, 1777, the General Assembly ordered to be paid the account of "John Kelly for the ferriage of soldiers." It amounted to £15 9s 4d. Michael Cary, "a private in the Rhode Island Continentals," is also mentioned in the records of the General Assembly. In September, 1779, the Assembly allowed a sum of money to Jeremiah Cain, "a soldier, to enable him to defray his expenses to Boston to join the corps of invalids at that place."

In July, 1780, the case of Philip Driskill, "enlisted by Richmond and claimed by Westerly," came up in the Assembly. He was finally credited to Richmond. Matthew Hanley, "late a soldier in the Continental army," was under discussion about the same time on a question of pension. He and Peter Burns are mentioned as invalids.

In the records of December, 1786, is found mention of "John Hany, age fifty-nine, who served in the Rhode Island regiment commanded by Colonel Jeremiah Olney." Hany was wounded in the ankle and groin. The former injury was received in May, 1780, and the latter in July, 1781. Both his heels were frost-bitten in the Oswego expedition. He is further described as suffering from "old age and bodily infirmity." Suitable provision was made for the worthy veteran. Other Rhode Islanders mentioned as of the "corps of invalids," at various times, were: John O'Neal, Daniel Barrett, John Griffin, and Edward Powers. In June, 1783, they were at Constitution Island. The Rhode Island Continentals participated in some of the leading battles of the Revolution. By act of congress Jan. 1, 1781, the 1st and 2d Continental regiments of the state were consolidated. Col. Christopher Greene was selected to command the organization. This led to the retirement of Col. Israel Angell. Colonel Greene was killed in May, 1781, and the command devolved upon Lieutenant-Colonel Olney. The latter led the regiment to the siege of Yorktown, 1781. A company from the regiment was in the van in the assault on the British redoubts. It was commanded by Capt. Stephen Olney. The regiment at this time included many Irish from Providence, Newport, and other parts of Rhode Island. The following soldiers were among those comprised in the regiment Feb. 1, 1781, or soon after: Dennis Hogan (sergeant), John Butler (sergeant), Michael Kelly, Cornelius Driskle, William Sullivan, Nicholas Hart, Matthew Hart, Michael Doherty, Peter Burns, James Hayes, Thomas Mitchell, Charles McAfferty, Michael Wright, John Kirby, Matthew Henley (or Hanley), Christopher Moore, Anthony Griffin, Daniel Collins, Peter Collins, William McCall, John Haney, James Mitchell, Thomas Melony (also spelled Maloney), Francis Cavan, Hugh McDonnold, and John McDonnold.

"CAPTAIN OLNEY'S COMPANY FORM HERE!"

Capt. Stephen Olney's company of the regiment, as has been stated, was placed in the van of one of the assaulting columns. It performed many deeds of valor, and was the one whose commander, having leaped upon the parapet of the redoubt, quickly called out: "Captain Olney's company form here!" Charles McAfferty, of the company, is mentioned[1] by Captain Olney as "an Irishman," which was a fact. McAfferty was a native of Londonderry, Ireland, and enlisted at Bristol, R. I., March 28, 1777, "for the war." In a regimental roll his age is given as 29 years. In a return he is mentioned as "On main guard, Morristown," March, 1780.

On sea as well as on land Irish Rhode Islanders dealt vigorous blows for the cause of Liberty. John Murphy of Rhode Island was a privateer commander during the Revolution. He was captain of the *Swallow*. William Malone was captain of the *Harbinger*. Francis Mulligan owned the *Chance*. Oliver Read was master of the privateer *General Rochambeau*; Peter Day of the *Molly's Adventure*; Thomas Jackson of the *Providence*; Richard Whellon [Whelon, Whalen?] of the *Broome*. M. Mackay is mentioned as owner of the privateer *Greyhound* during the Revolution. He is believed to have been a resident, at one period, of Newport.

Among the patriots captured in privateers and imprisoned in England were: Stephen Ready, John Welch, Edward McGrath, William Kelly, John Murphy, and Charles Buckley. They are all thought to have been of Rhode Island.

A census of men in Rhode Island, able or unable to bear arms, was taken in 1777, in accordance with an Act of the General Assembly. This Act required that there should be ascertained (1) The number of men from six-

---

[1] See letter by Captain Olney in Stone's *Our French Allies*.

teen to fifty years of age able to bear arms. (2) The number from sixteen to fifty unable to bear arms. (3) The number from fifty to sixty able to bear arms. (4) The number from fifty to sixty not able to bear arms, and (5) the number from sixty upwards.

A copy of the returns from this census may be consulted at the state record commissioner's office, in the capitol, at Providence. It contains, among many others, the following names, the bearers of which are all described as "able": Stephen Burk, James Boyd, Thomas Cain, Stephen Cummins, Thomas Cummins, James Currey, John Driskill, Richard Ford, William Ford, Joseph Hart, John Heffernan, Stephen Heffernan, Michael Johnson, Stephen Killey, John Larkin, Timothy Larkin, Peter Lee, James Martin, Jeremiah M'Coy, Michael McDonald, James Mead, David Moore, Daniel Ray, Joseph Ray, Ferrel Ryley, Fenner Ryley, William Strange and John Welch.

IRISH SERVING UNDER ESEK HOPKINS.

Mr. Edward Field's work on *Esek Hopkins, Commander-in-chief of the Continental Navy, 1775 to 1778*, mentions a number of Irish names as borne, at that period, by American sailors and marines. These were not necessarily Rhode Islanders, though some of them may have been. Among other names Mr. Field mentions Anthony Dwyer, Richard Sweeney, Patrick Kaine, Thomas Doyle, John Connor, Andrew Magee, Thomas Dowd, John Roatch, and George Kennedy. Of these Dwyer, Sweeney, Dowd, Connor, Magee and Roatch signed a "round robin" petition to Hopkins, at one time, asking for back pay. They were of the armed vessel *Cabot*. Kaine, Doyle and Kennedy—marines—were also of the *Cabot*. In a conflict April 6, 1776, with the British ship *Glasgow*, Doyle was wounded, and Kaine and Kennedy were killed. The *Cabot* is mentioned at one time as bringing into Newport, R. I., twenty-six guns captured at the Bahamas.

Captain Melally commanded a privateer in the Revolution. A better known form of this Irish name would be Mullally. The captain was with his ship in Newport harbor soon after the evacuation by the British. While riding at anchor there he noticed entering the harbor, one evening, the British sloop *Crawford*. The latter's commander supposed the place to be still held by the British. General Cornell was in command of the port, and had given orders that while no boat should be hailed coming in from the sea, none should be allowed to go out without a certificate or pass.

As soon as the British vessel had got safely inside, Captain Melally manned one of his boats, sent her aboard the stranger, and took possession of the astounded visitor. Melally's claim to the vessel was disputed on the ground that the British vessel was "within the limits, jurisdiction, and presidium of the state." It was also claimed that Captain Melally's power to make captures could not "extend to any place, extra presidia of the guns, power and jurisdiction of a state." J. M. Varnum accordingly libeled the *Crawford* in behalf of the state and obtained a decree, whereupon Captain Melally appealed to the Congress from the decision.

Luke Burns, a cordwainer, was a resident of Providence. He died early in 1788. Jonathan Green, "living near the Mill-Bridge in Providence," was made administrator of his estate. Among deaths in Providence, during the Revolution, we find mention of Lawrence Kelly, who died in March, 1777; James Madden, April, 1777; Basil Reily, January, 1779; and James Burke, July, 1779. These men, if not active participants, at least witnessed many stirring events of the Revolution.

COL. ISRAEL ANGELL ON ST. PATRICK'S DAY.

In the diary of Col. Israel Angell of the Second Rhode Island regiment, in the Continental line, is found the following interesting entry under date of March 17, 1781: "Good weather. A great parade this day with the Irish it being St. Patrick's. I spent the day on the Point [West Point] and tarried with the officers."

John Fitton, a native of the city of Waterford, Ireland, was a resident of Providence during the Revolution. He settled here about 1750-'51, and was a resident of the town for about sixty years, dying in 1810. He was a merchant. The year of his birth was 1731. Faril Reily was another Irish resident of Providence, a trader, and accumulated considerable property. He died in 1779, during the Revolution. The administrators of his estate were Jane Reily, Theodore Foster and Terence Reily.

Patrick Mackey came from Philadelphia to Providence. In 1768 he opened "a skinner's shop near the Hayward on the east side of the great bridge." George Taylor, an Irishman, became a prominent resident of Providence. He died in 1778, in the seventy-seventh year of his age. The Providence *Gazette* states that "he was an honor to the country that gave him birth." Taylor taught school in Providence for over forty years, was for a number of years president of the town council, and held other offices of trust and honor. He was a man of great public spirit, and witnessed leading events of the earlier part of the Revolution. A number of French officers of Irish birth or descent came to Rhode Island, in 1780, with the forces landing at Newport. Stone in his work on *Our French Allies*, referring to Newport, mentions Count Arthur Dillon who was colonel of the Regiment of Dillon. Mention is also made of Isidore de Lynch, then aide-de-camp to the Chevalier de Chastellux. Referring to the return of the French to Boston after the fall of Yorktown, Count Ségur speaks of "Isidore de Lynch, an intrepid Irishman, afterwards a General." Lynch became commander of the Irish-French regiment of Walsh, and was decorated with the Cross of St. Louis. Colonel, the Count Dillon abovementioned, came of a famous Irish family. He was accompanied to America by a kinsman, Lieut.-Col. Barthelemy Dillon, who was born in Ireland, 1729, and who married the widow of the Marquis de Montlezun. Count Dillon later became a general of brigade and maréchal-de-camp. He fell a victim to the Terror, and perished by the guillotine in the Place de la Revolution, Paris. Theobald Dillon, another of the count's kinsmen, entered the Regiment of Dillon [1] as a cadet in 1761. He was a native of Ireland, saw service in America, was a member of the Cincinnati, and subsequently became a brigadier-general in France. Matthew Dillon, a kinsman, is also mentioned as serving in America.[2]

[1] *Archives de la Guerre*, Paris. *Mercure Francais*, 1792. *Annuaire de la Noblesse.*

Observations historiques sur l'origine les services et l'etat civil des officiers Irlandois au service de la France. Redigées par M. A. D. député à l' Assemblée Nationale. (Pamphlet attributed to Count Arthur Dillon, and published about 1789.)

[2] For an historical account of the Regiment of Dillon see O'Callaghan's *History of the Irish Brigades in the Service of France.*

Another officer serving with our allies was Captain Commandant O'Neil. He was of the fifth generation of those who served the French king in the Regiment of Dillon[1] " since the passage of Irishmen into France." O'Neil was in the expedition against Savannah, where he was wounded in the breast.

Another Irishman who held a commission in the army of France was Edward Stack. He came to America with our allies and rendered valiant service. He was probably the officer named Stack who arrived at Newport with Rochambeau's forces, in 1780, and who is mentioned as aide to Viscount de Viomesnil. Stack had quarters on Spring street, in Newport, at the house of William Almy.

Captain James Shee, Captain Macdonnall, Captain Mullens, Lieutenant Taaffe and Lieutenant O'Farrell also served in America with the French. Shee was born in Ireland, Feb. 15, 1735. Taaffe was likewise a native of

[1] Among the commanders of the Regiment of Dillon, at different periods, may be mentioned: Colonel, the Hon. Arthur Dillon, 1690; colonel, the Count Charles Dillon, 1730; colonel, the Count Henry Dillon, 1741; colonel, the Chevalier James Dillon, 1744; colonel, the Count Edward Dillon, 1745; colonel, the Count Arthur Dillon, 1747; colonel, the Count Theobald Dillon, 1767. Each of the foregoing was a "Colonel Proprietor."

Among other officers who are recorded as having been of the Regiment of Dillon were: Denis O'Callaghan, captain, 1698; Laurence Bourke, captain, 1707; Charles O'Neill, lieutenant, 1721-'26; Captain O'Connor, 1723; Edward Fitz Gerald, lieutenant, 1730 (Maréchal-de-Camp, 1762); Michael Sheridan, colonel, 1742 (became a major-general of cavalry); Edward Reilly, captain, 1745; John McDonough, lieutenant, 1745; Captain Magenis, 1745, Bernard Magennis, lieutenant, 1757; James P. O'Flannagan, lieutenant-colonel, 1766 (a chevalier of St. Louis); Joseph L. O'Hurley, captain, 1756-'80 (a chevalier of St. Louis); Patrick O'Kelly, captain, 1774-'79 (a chevalier of St. Louis); Daniel O'Carroll, captain, 1775-'79 (a chevalier of St. Louis); Le Baron Bernard O'Neill, captain, 1777 (a chevalier of St. Louis); Lieutenant-Colonel O'Mahoney, 1778 (a chevalier of St. Louis); Daniel O'Sullivan, captain, 1778; Denis O'Sullivan, captain, 1778; P. F. McGuire, captain, 1779-'83 (a chevalier of St. Louis); Michael McDermott, captain, 1779 (a chevalier of St. Louis). Some of the latter of these officers may have been in Rhode Island with our French allies.

Ireland, and was born in 1757. He was killed at Savannah, 1779. O'Farrell, of the Regiment of Dillon, was wounded in the assault on Savannah. Mullens, of the Irish-French Regiment of Berwick, saw much service in America, and was at one time a "Captain des Guides." Stone, in *Our French Allies*, mentions an officer named Mullins, who was at Newport with Rochambeau's forces in 1780. He had quarters there, at the house of Mrs. Mumford, and the fact that he is described as a "Captain des Guides" leads to the conviction that he and the Captain Mullens here mentioned were identical. Macdonnall, of the Regiment of Dillon, took part in the movement against Savannah. At one time during the operations he had command of a picket of sixty volunteers.

TWO OTHER NOTED IRISH-FRENCH SOLDIERS.

Two other noted soldiers who served in America under Rochambeau were Charles Geoghegan[1] and James O'Moran. The former was an Irishman, a native of the County Westmeath. He received the decoration of the Cincinnati from the hands of Washington, returned to France and was made a general.[2] O'Moran was also an Irishman,

---

[1] Pronounced *Gay-gen*.

[2] Many thousands of men of Irish blood have served in the armies of France. In 1690, France having forwarded seven battalions to James II, in Ireland, the latter sent a number of Irish regiments, including Dillon's, O'Brien's and Mountcashel's, to the French King. Eventually each of these regiments comprised 1,600 men, divided into 16 companies. Finer corps were never seen in Europe. This was the first Irish brigade in the service of France and was commanded by Mountcashel (Justin MacCarthy). After the fall of Limerick, in 1691, nearly 20,000 Irish troops enlisted in the French service. In 1695 there were in France about a dozen Irish regiments, including some of the finest cavalry in the service. For more than a century the Irish brigades reflected glory upon the shamrock and the lilies. Many of the Irish commanders attained eminent rank in the French service. High orders were conferred upon them. Thus, Count Patrick Darcy became a Knight of St. Louis and of St. Lazarus ; Count Arthur Lally became a Knight Grand Cross of St. Louis ;

born in 1739, and attained eminence in France. He, likewise, was enrolled in the Cincinnati. At the close of the war in America he returned to France and became a major-general. He was brought before the revolutionary tribunal in France and perished, like Dillon, at the hands of the Terror. Whether Geoghegan and O'Moran were ever in Rhode Island the writer cannot say. If not at Newport, it is possible they may have accompanied the French army on its return through Rhode Island from Yorktown.

M. de McCarty was another Irish-French officer at Newport, R. I. He was attached to the battleship *Le Conquerant*,[1] and is recorded as an "Ensigne de Vaisseau." Some of the chaplains who accompanied the French forces to America were also Irish, selected because of their ability to speak the language of the country. The names of two of these—Lacy[2] and Whelan[3]—have come down to us. Whether they were at Newport is not known, though it is by no means improbable.

Maurice MacMahon, a Knight of Malta; Jacques Francois Edouard Sarsfield (descendant of Patrick Sarsfield), a Knight of the Golden Fleece; Charles O'Brien, a marshal of France. One soldier of Irish descent—MacMahon—became, even in our own day, president of France.

[1] Stone's *Our French Allies*.

[2] Journal of Claude Blanchard.

[3] The Rev. Charles Whelan was an Irish Franciscan. At the close of the Revolution he ministered to a congregation in New York city, and subsequently labored on the Kentucky mission. He died in Maryland in 1809.

MEN FROM MASSACHUSETTS SERVING IN RHODE ISLAND.

MANY soldiers of Irish extraction came to Rhode Island from Massachusetts, and saw service here, at various periods during the Revolution. The rolls in the Bay state archives[1] bear evidence of this fact.

In some instances these men are spoken of as responding to "an alarm" from Rhode Island, as assembling for "a secret expedition" to the state or as being stationed here as a portion of the patriot army under General Sullivan and other commanders.

Rolls signed by State or Continental "Muster Masters" are still in existence and may be consulted relative to this subject. Pay abstracts "sworn to in quarters at Providence" or elsewhere are also found as well as muster rolls "dated Providence" and at other places. In fact, the Massachusetts records contain a great deal of valuable data in this respect.

Reference has already been made to Hon. James Sullivan, a brother of Gen. John Sullivan, who participated with the latter in the battle of Rhode Island, August 29, 1778. James was then a judge of the superior court of Massachusetts, and subsequently became governor of that state. Brown University conferred upon him the degree LL. D.

[1] See *Massachusetts Soldiers and Sailors of the Revolutionary War. A Compilation from the Archives, Prepared and Published by the Secretary of the Commonwealth.* (Boston.)

Lieut. Patrick Phelon was of Col. David Henley's Massachusetts regiment, and is mentioned in a return dated Providence, September 11, 1778. He was transferred to Jackson's Massachusetts regiment in April, 1779, and early in 1781 was transferred to the Ninth Massachusetts, serving in 1783 in the Third Massachusetts. He was a captain in the Second U. S. Infantry, 1791, and was killed November 4 that year in an engagement with Indians at St. Clair's defeat near Fort Recovery, Ohio.

Ensign Edward Phelon, of Henley's regiment, was in camp at Pawtuxet, R. I., October 10, 1778. He subsequently served in Jackson's regiment and in other Massachusetts commands. He is mentioned as a lieutenant, October 14, 1781, and as captain September 30, 1783. He died January 7, 1810.

Lieut. John Phelan, another Massachusetts officer, was at Providence in 1778 and 1779. His name is also spelled Phelon. He participated in the battle of Rhode Island and was wounded in that engagement. He served to November 3, 1783, and died in September, 1827.

Timothy Sullivan, of Captain Cushing's company, Col. Joseph Vose's regiment, was stationed at Providence in 1779.

John O'Brian, a Massachusetts soldier, was in an "expedition to Rhode Island," in 1778.

Sergt. James O'Bryant (probably O'Brien or O'Bryan), was of Capt. Ezra Lunt's company, Henley's regiment. His name appears in a return sworn to at Providence, September, 1778.

Thomas Obryan, of Capt. Abraham Hunt's company, Vose's regiment, was stationed at Providence in 1779.

Ralph O'Daniels, of Capt. Ephraim Lyon's company,

Colonel Wade's regiment, is credited with service "at Rhode Island" in 1778.

Lieut. John Gilpatrick was of Capt. Joseph Pray's company, Wade's regiment, stationed in the state of Rhode Island, 1778.

Lieut. John Gillpatrick, Jr., was a Massachusetts soldier located with his company at East Greenwich, R. I. He was a grandson of Thomas and Margaret Gillpatrick, who came from Ireland in 1720, and settled in what is now Kennebunk, Me.

Richard Shean was of Captain Pray's company, in Colonel Wade's regiment, and was serving in Rhode Island during the latter half of 1778.

John Welch was also of Wade's regiment, serving in the same company as Richard Shean, just mentioned.

Eben, or Ebenezer, Sullivan, brother of Gen. John Sullivan, took part in the battle of Rhode Island and acquired an honorable record as an officer during the war. He had been educated for the bar, but early enlisted in the military service of his country. He was a captain in Scammon's Massachusetts regiment, May to December, 1775, and was, later, a captain in the Fifteenth Continental infantry. Taken prisoner at the Cedars, May 20, 1776, he was exchanged in 1778.

The following is a list of

SOME MASSACHUSETTS MEN SERVING IN RHODE ISLAND.

Barr, Hugh
Barrett, James
Barrey, John
Bennett, Jeremiah
Bennett, Joseph
Blake, James
Blake, Jeremiah
Blake, John
Brown, Patrick
Boyle, John

Burk, Anthony
Burk, John
Burk, Richard
Burk, William
Burns, William
Cane, John
Cary, Daniel
Casady, William
Casey, Edward
Casey, John
Cassady, Michael
Cochran, John
Conery, Peter
Conner, John
Connolly, William
Connor, Joseph
Conway, William
Cook, Matthew
Cowen, Patrick
Crowley, Abraham
Curry, Henry
Daily, David
Daily, Lewis
Daley, Daniel
Daley, Nathaniel
Daley, Peter
Donnagan, Cornelius
Dowd, Isaac
Driskill, Joseph
Dunn, John
Dunn, Thomas
Fay, Thomas
Fitz Gerald, Michael
Fitzgerrl, James
Flood, Stephen
Ford, Benjamin
Ford, Mark
Ford, Robert

Gilligan, Matthew
Gilligan, Thomas
Gilpatrick, John
Gillpatrick, John, Jr.
Gillpatrick, Nathaniel
Ginness, Benjamin
Gleason, Daniel
Gleason, John
Gleason, Joseph
Jordan, John
Jordan, Martin
Keef, William
Keley, David
Keley, Hugh
Kelley, John
Kelley, Morris
Kelley, Robert
Kelley, Stephen
Kelly, David
Kelly, Timothy
Kelly, William
Kenedy, John,
Keney, Samuel
Kennedy, John
Kennedy, William
Kennelly, Alex
Kenney, Daniel
Kenney, John
Kenney, Stephen
Kenney, Timothy
Kenney, William
Kenny, John
Kenny, Thomas
Knox, Henry
Lane, Daniel
Larkin, Edmund
Linihan, William
Long, Matthew

Lyon, Michael	McMullen, John
Madden, Michael	McMullen, William
Mahan, John	McNeal, Francis
Mallon, James	McNeal, John
McBride, William	Melony, John
McCarty, Dennis	Moore, Timothy
McCormick, James	Obryan, Thomas
McCoy, Barnabus	O'Brian, John
McCoy, Peter	O'Bryant, James
McCurtin, William	O'Daniels, Ralph
McDermit, Patrick	Phelan, John
McElroy, Robert	Phelon, Edward
McGlaughlin, Owen	Phelon, Patrick
McLarey, James	Shean, Richard
McLouth, Lawrence, Jr.	Sullivan, Ebenezer
McLouth, Lewis	Sullivan, James
McLouth, Peter	Sullivan, Timothy
McLouth, Solomon	Sullivan, William
McMickel, James	Welch, John

WAS IN "GARRISON AT PAWTUXET."

Patrick Brown, of the foregoing list of Massachusetts men, is mentioned as of Weymouth, Mass. He saw much service at different points during the war. He was in Col. Henry Jackson's regiment. At one time (April, 1779) his name appears in a muster roll dated "Garrison at Pawtuxet." His name also appears in a return dated Providence, July 8, 1779, and in a return from the "Camp at Providence," Dec. 31, 1779.

Anthony Burk was at one time of a company raised "for a secret expedition to Rhode Island," the company's service at that time being given as thirty-seven days. He also served during the war in other commands. His occupation is given as "husbandman," and his nationality, "Irish."

John Burk, of Brookfield, Mass., was a Continental soldier. He is mentioned in a pay abstract for November, 1778, "sworn to in quarters at Providence." He was of Colonel Sheppard's regiment, and his name also appears in a muster roll for March and April, 1779, "dated Providence."

Edward Casey was of Col. Ebenezer Thayer's regiment (Suffolk county, Mass.). He served three months and eight days "at Rhode Island." He enlisted July 26, 1780.

John Casey enlisted Aug. 13, 1779. He was of Capt. Edward Hammond's company. His period of service "at Rhode Island" is given as one month and seven days.

Michael Cassady, of Boston, served in Col. Joseph Vose's Continental regiment. He was at Valley Forge and, later, at Providence. His name appears in a muster roll for November, 1778, "dated Providence"; also in an "order for gratuity," dated Providence, Feb. 13, 1779, and in a muster roll for March and April, 1779, "dated Providence."

John Conner served in Col. John Fellows' regiment and likewise in that of Col. William Sheppard. He was in Providence in 1778 and 1779, and perhaps at other periods. He was of the Continental line.

Joseph Connor was a private, and served in Rhode Island under Major William Rogers. At various periods during the war he was of Capt. Jonathan Poor's company, and also of that of Capt. Benjamin Pike.

William Connolly, of Boston, served in Col. Henry Jackson's regiment, and is mentioned as of Lieutenant Bayley's company of grenadiers in that command. His name appears in various returns in 1778 and 1779, dated "Camp at Providence," and Pawtuxet.

Patrick Cowen, of Dedham, Mass., served in Col. Benjamin Hawes' regiment. In 1777 his company participated in a "secret expedition to Rhode Island." He also served in Col. Samuel Pierce's regiment. In 1779 Cowen was on duty at Tiverton, R. I. He was likewise, during the war, of Col. Nathan Tyler's regiment, and is also mentioned as of Major Nathaniel Heath's "detachment of guards."

Martin Jordan, of this Massachusetts list, was a native of Cork, Ireland. He became a resident of West Springfield, Mass., and served in Col. Joseph Vose's regiment. His name appears on muster rolls "sworn to at Providence," 1778-'79.

Timothy Kenney was detached from Colonel Gill's regiment for service under Capt. John Armstrong on an expedition to Rhode Island.

Thomas Kenny was a drummer; served in Col. Calvin Smith's regiment; was at Valley Forge. He is mentioned in a pay-roll, 1778, "sworn to at Providence," and in a muster roll, March and April, 1779, "dated Providence."

Stephen Kenney responded to "an alarm at Rhode Island." He was of Capt. Jonathan Woodbury's company, in Col. Jacob Davis' regiment, 1780.

Daniel Kenney's name appears in a list, dated Boston, Feb. 11, 1779, detached from Col. Jacob Hatch's (Boston) regiment by Brig.-Gen. Lovell to serve at Providence.

Cornelius Donnagan, a matross in Col. John Crane's artillery regiment. The name appears in muster rolls, 1779, dated Providence and Tiverton. He enlisted March 24, 1778, for three years.

Joseph Driskill, a lieutenant in Col. John Crane's artillery regiment; also in Stevens' corps of artillery. Lieutenant Driskill is mentioned in a "return for gratuity dated Greenwich, Nov. 10, 1779."

Thomas Gilligan, of Colonel Wigglesworth's regiment; his name appears in a muster roll dated Providence, March and April, 1779. He was of Western (Warren), Mass., and enlisted March 6, 1777, for three years.

Micah [Michael?] Fitz Gerald, a private in Captain Howard's company. Roll dated Bridgewater, Mass. The company "marched to Rhode Island on the alarm of July 30, 1780." The Massachusetts rolls also mention Michael Fittsgereld, Michael Fitz Jerrell, Michael Fitzjerld, Michael Fitzgerold and Michael Fitzjerrill. These names may have referred to the same individual.

Matthew Gilligin, credited to the town of Western (Warren), Mass.; served in Col. Calvin Smith's regiment ("late Wigglesworth's"); Gilligin's name appears in a muster roll, July, 1778, "dated Camp Greenwich," and in one for March and April, 1779, dated Providence.

NEW HAMPSHIRE MEN IN RHODE ISLAND.

THE most prominent New Hampshire man who rendered service in Rhode Island during the Revolution was, of course, Gen. John Sullivan. He was commissioned a brigadier-general by the Congress, took part in the siege of Boston and by his own exertions raised 2,000 New Hampshire men, who also participated in the siege.

The British evacuated Boston on St. Patrick's Day, March 17, 1776. Soon after this event, Sullivan, with his brigade, was ordered to Rhode Island to repel a threatened attack by the enemy. Sullivan and Greene, the latter a native of Warwick, R. I., were commissioned major-generals on the same day, became close friends and were associated on many important occasions.

On the recommendation of Greene and Washington, General Sullivan was appointed by the Congress to succeed General Spencer as commander of the Rhode Island department. Under date of Providence, March 30, 1778, Gov. Nicholas Cooke of Rhode Island thus wrote to Sullivan:

"SIR:—I am favored with yours of the 26th informing me of your appointment to the command of the troops in this state. I have the pleasure of informing you that the appointment is highly satisfactory to us, and we hope will prove equally beneficial to the public and glorious to you."

In May, 1778, the General Assembly of Rhode Island "*Resolved*, That it be recommended to the Hon. Major-

General Sullivan, to take up all persons who are suspected or known to be unfriendly to the state, or to the United States in general, that he shall think proper, and proceed against them according to the known practice in such cases in the army under the immediate command of His Excellency General Washington."

Many officers and men from New Hampshire, of Irish blood, served in Rhode Island at different periods. In the roll of Lieut.-Col. Joseph Senter's force, of the Granite state, which was " marched to Rhode Island " in 1777, we find such names as Samuel Haley, William Kelley, Arthur Molloy, Humphrey Flood, John Gowen, James Neal, Eliphalet O'Conner and a number of others that might be cited.

Under date of Warwick, R. I., Nov. 18, 1777, Colonel Senter wrote to the New Hampshire authorities, stating that he arrived at Providence, R. I., Sept. 12, that year, and waited upon General Spencer, who gave him an order Sept. 14 to march to Warwick and serve under Cornell. The latter at once put Senter's force at work building a fort and guarding the shore. On Sept. 21 Cornell informed Senter that an expedition was planned against the enemy at Newport. He then ordered Senter to take command of the post and to collect all the boats on the shore from East Greenwich to Pawtuxet and put them in repair. Senter was also ordered to supply the militia, as soon as the latter came in, with cartridges and flints and to send the militia across the Providence river at night, that the movement might not be discovered by the enemy. On Oct. 8, 1777, Senter with his men crossed the river to Warren, R. I. Oct. 10 he marched to Swanzey; Oct. 12, to Tiverton; Oct. 14, to Little Compton. The expedition, however, was a failure, owing to its premature discovery by the British.

Gen. John Stark was another distinguished soldier who served in Rhode Island. His father was a native of Scotland, who went over to Ireland, where he married Eleanor Nichols, a native of the Irish province of Ulster, and subsequently came to America. John, the future general, was born in the Irish settlement of Londonderry,[1] N. H., Aug. 28, 1728. Mackenzie, a biographer of General Stark, in speaking[2] of the latter's victory at Bennington, calls special attention to the fact that the general was the "son of an Irish mother."

GENERAL SULLIVAN WRITES TO THE CONGRESS.

On May 3, 1778, General Sullivan, then in command of the Rhode Island department, wrote to the Congress, saying: "As the number of troops destined for this department will be so incompetent to defend it against a sudden attack, I think that the two State galleys, if properly fitted, would be of great advantage. . . . I also beg Congress to order Gen. Stark, who has returned to New Hampshire from Albany, to me at this place, as I shall need two brigadiers when the troops arrive; and the more so, as the extent of country to guard will be so great."

General Stark was accordingly ordered to Rhode Island, and late in 1778 reached Providence. He was cordially

---

[1] Rev. James MacSparran, an Irish Protestant clergyman of Rhode Island, writing in 1752 and referring to New Hampshire says, "In this province lies that town called London-Derry, all Irish, and famed for industry and riches."

[2] William L. Mackenzie's *The Sons of the Emerald Isle or Lives of One Thousand Remarkable Irishmen; including Memoirs of Noted Characters of Irish Parentage or Descent.* (New York city, 1844.)

welcomed and was soon assigned to take post at East Greenwich on the west shore of Narragansett Bay. Here he became very popular with the militia, who admired his soldierly and democratic qualities. Upon the close of his duties at that point, he went back to New Hampshire to raise recruits and needed supplies.

He came to Rhode Island again in the spring of 1779, and was ordered to watch the coast from Providence to Point Judith on the west side of the bay, and from Providence to Mount Hope on the east side. He was almost constantly in the saddle and seldom rested more than one night in the same place. Upon the evacuation of Newport by the British, General Stark marched in and took possession.

A New Hampshire brigade, under Gen. William Whipple, came to Rhode Island in 1778. Among the officers accompanying it were: Col. Moses Kelly, Capt. James Gilmore, Capt. Daniel Moore, Lieut. Robert McMurphy, Lieut. James Garven, Lieut. James Hackett and others bearing Irish names. Colonel Kelly commanded a regiment in the brigade. He belonged in Goffstown, N. H., and owned mills there at the locality now called "Kelly's Falls." Lieut. James Hackett, just mentioned, was a shipbuilder at Portsmouth, N. H. He was second in command of a company of Light Horse that volunteered for this expedition to Rhode Island, John Langdon being captain of the company. The latter numbered forty-six men, rank and file.

COLONEL MOONEY'S NEW HAMPSHIRE REGIMENT.

Early in 1779 a New Hampshire regiment, commanded by Col. Hercules Mooney, was ordered to Rhode Island.

Colonel Mooney was of Lee, N. H. He was a member of the Committee of Safety, 1778-1779, and in 1782 was a member of the New Hampshire legislature. Among the officers of his regiment when the latter was ordered to Rhode Island were: Major Daniel Reynolds, Quartermaster Timothy Gleason and Lieut. Samuel Kelly.

Capt. William Scott, another New Hampshire officer of Irish descent, served under General Sullivan in Rhode Island and remained with the army until 1781, when he entered the naval service.

Among those who served in Rhode Island as members of Col. Moses Nichols' New Hampshire regiment were: Thomas Curry, John Moore, James Johnson, John McClure, Moses Welch, Thomas Cowen, Daniel Kenney, Daniel Downing, Joseph Johnson and Thomas Moore.

In Col. Enoch Hale's New Hampshire regiment serving in Rhode Island, there were among others: John Mellen, Charles McCoy, John McBride, and William McCoy.

In Colonel Kelly's New Hampshire regiment, during its service in Rhode Island, were: Thomas Mitchell, John Cochran, Philip Johnson, John Burns, William Moore, John McClary, William Burns and John McMillan.

Lieut.-Col. Stephen Peabody's regiment, raised by the state of New Hampshire "for the Continental service at Rhode Island," 1778, included Joseph Tate, Daniel Lary, Paul Blake, James Lane, and William Kelly. Of these, Lary, Blake and Kelly were in Capt. Samuel Dearborn's company of the regiment.

Among other New Hampshire soldiers who served in Rhode Island, mention is found of John McCarty, Joseph Welch, William Boyd, Nathaniel Kelley, Neal McGee and Jeremiah Neal.

CONNECTICUT MEN IN RHODE ISLAND.

THE Connecticut troops serving in Rhode Island also included, like those from Massachusetts and New Hampshire, many who were of Irish birth or extraction.

Col. Samuel Chapman's regiment from Connecticut took part in the battle of Rhode Island, August 29, 1778, serving in the brigade of Gen. John Tyler. In the rolls of Chapman's regiment appear such names as Richard Butler, Denis Fling, Daniel Miles, James Morrison, Timothy Buckley and others indicative of Hibernian origin. Butler, Fling and Miles were of Captain Pomeroy's company of the regiment, while Morrison and Buckley were of Captain Olcott's company.

Col. Obadiah Johnson's Connecticut regiment was stationed in Providence, R. I., early in 1778, and had in its ranks a number of men bearing Irish names. Among these were: Michael Flynn, Stephen Brady, Matthew Reed, David Kenedy, James Keeney, William Carey, Thomas Raney, James McClure, Thomas Day and others.

Thomas Melona [Maloney], a Connecticut soldier, was killed in the battle of Rhode Island. This name appears in the rolls of Col. Samuel B. Webb's Connecticut regiment. The latter command wintered in Rhode Island in 1778–'79, and remained in the state until the fall of 1779, when it marched to winter quarters at Morristown, N. J. The regiment was raised for the Continental line.

John Riley, of Wethersfield, Conn., was a captain in the regiment; Stephen Buckley was a sergeant, and among others in the command were: Thomas Quigley, Benjamin Mack, Peter Butler, Thomas Doyle, Timothy Fay, Daniel Gilmore, George O'Bryan and Timothy Higgins.

SOME INTERESTING GENERAL MENTION.

IN December, 1777, the General Assembly of Rhode Island appointed John Reynolds agent for the clothing department " agreeably to the request of James Mease, Esq., Clothier-General of the Continental Army." Mease was an Irishman, a native of Strabane, and became prominent as a merchant in Philadelphia. In June, 1780, he subscribed £5,000 in aid of the patriot cause.

John Jenckes and Welcome Arnold, a committee, reported to the Rhode Island General Assembly in May, 1780, that among other goods in the stores of the state were "thirty yards and one quarter of Irish linen." The Rhode Island records of that period mention a number of interesting facts relative to people of Irish birth or descent.

In 1777, Thomas Burke was a member of the Marine Committee of Congress which sent a communication to Rhode Island's Council of War urging promptness in getting to sea the frigates of the state.

Daniel Carroll of Maryland, cousin to Charles Carroll of Carrollton, was appointed president of the Congress in November, 1781, during the illness of the regular presiding officer. On that and other occasions he had more or less official relations with Rhode Island. In 1782-'83, Rhode Island refused to vest congress with power to levy an impost tax of five per cent. Daniel Carroll was on a committee to consider Rhode Island's claim in this respect.

The distinguished naval officer, John Barry, was in Rhode Island at various times during the Revolution. Barry was a native of County Wexford, Ireland, his boyhood's home standing close by the sea. In 1775, the Congress gave him command of the *Lexington*. In 1778, he received the rank of commodore. He defeated the British in various engagements, and received the thanks of Washington and of the Congress. In July, 1783, he is noted as departing from Providence on his frigate the *Alliance,* for Virginia, from whence he proceeded to Europe.

Blair McClenachan, another patriot of Irish birth, subscribed £10,000 in aid of the Revolution. He was a leading merchant in Philadelphia, a member of the Hibernia Fire company, of that city, and of the Hibernian Society. In a discussion with David Howell of Rhode Island, who was a member of the Continental Congress, 1782 to 1785, McClenachan warmly praised Rhode Island's course in the impost matter. (See Staples' *Rhode Island in the Continental Congress.*) McClenachan became a member of the Pennsylvania Assembly, and of the National House of Representatives. He died in 1812.

Nathaniel Greene, John Sullivan and Henry Knox, the two latter of Irish parentage, were intimate associates in the camp at Cambridge, Mass. Mrs. Greene, Mrs. Knox and the wives of other officers brightened the camp by their presence. There were many enjoyable social events. A note written at the time reads: "General Greene and lady present their compliments to Colonel Knox and his lady, and should be glad of their company to-morrow at two o'clock."

On one occasion, while General Sullivan was in command of the Rhode Island department, General Greene wrote him as follows: "By a letter this moment received from Major Cortland, I find I am not to have the pleasure of your company to dine with us to-day. Should be glad to know when you can make it convenient."

Gen. Anthony Wayne, whose father was a native of Ireland, was a great friend of Gen. Nathaniel Greene, and was by the latter's bedside when General Greene died in June, 1786. After Greene had passed away, Wayne wrote: "My dear friend, General Greene, is no more. He was great as a soldier, greater as a citizen, immaculate as a friend. Pardon this scrawl; my feelings are too much affected because I have seen a great and good man die." General Wayne was a member of the Friendly Sons of St. Patrick, Philadelphia, Pa., and of the Hibernian Society of that city.

AN INDEX OF PLACES.

Albany, N. Y., 69.
American Colonies, 5, 6.
Antrim, Ire., 31.
Armagh, Ire., 34.
Bahamas, 53.
Barbadoes, 5.
Barrington, R. I., 13, 31, 39, 40.
"Bay," The, 4, 5.
Belfast, Ire., 33.
Bennington, Vt., 69.
Berwick, Me., 10.
Boston, Mass., 4, 9, 48, 49, 55, 59, 64, 65, 67.
Brefney, Ire., 37.
Bristol, R. I., 28, 34. 43, 51.
Bridgewater, Mass., 66.
Brookfield, Mass., 63.
Brookline, Mass., 6.
Cambridge, Mass., 21, 74.
Canada, 20, 29, 36.
Carlow, Ire., 33.
Carrollton, Md., 73.
Cavan, Ire., 37.
Ceara, Ire., 37.
Centreville, R. I., 24.
Connacht, Ire., 6.
Connecticut, 5, 6, 7, 72.
Constitution Island, 42, 50.
Cork, Ire., 5, 19, 34, 65.
Coventry, R. I., 33, 40.
Cumberland, R. I., 47.
Dedham, Mass., 64.
Donegal, Ire., 20, 35.
Drogheda, Ire., 33.
Dublin, Ire., 28, 33, 34.
Dunluce, Ire., 37.
Dunmanway, Ire., 37.

Dunmore, Ire., 37.
East Greenwich, R. I., 31, 61, 65, 66, 68, 70.
England, 5, 7, 51.
Exeter, R. I., 38.
Fort Island, 10, 43.
Fort Mercer, 23.
Fort Recovery, O., 60.
Fort Washington, 40.
Foster, R. I., 18.
France, 33, 55, 56, 57, 58.
Freetown, Mass., 23.
Galway, N. Y., 32.
Goffstown, N. H., 70.
Harlem Heights, 43.
Holland, 4.
Hopkinton, R. I., 44, 48.
Ireland, 6, 17, 19, 20, 21, 28, 31, 32, 33, 34, 35, 37, 41, 42, 43, 44, 55, 56, 57, 61, 69, 73.
Jamaica, 5.
Kennebunk, Me., 61.
Kent County, R. I., 27.
Kentucky, 58.
Kildare, Ire., 33.
Kilkenny, Ire., 28, 29, 33.
Kinsale, Ire., 5, 34.
Lee, N. H., 71.
Leinster, Ire., 6.
Leitrim, Ire., 37.
Lexington, Mass., 31.
Limerick, Ire., 28, 29, 33, 34, 57.
Little Compton, R. I., 68.
Londonderry, Ire., 20, 51.
Londonderry, N. H., 20, 69.
Maryland, 4, 58, 73.

Massachusetts, 4, 37, 59, 60, 61, 65, 72.
Mayo, Ire., 37.
Meath, Ire., 33, 37.
Morristown, N. J., 72.
Mountmellick, Ire., 33.
Muddy River, Mass., 6.
Munster, Ire., 6.
Narragansett Bay, 70.
New England, 5, 6, 22.
New Hampshire, 46, 67, 68, 69, 70, 71, 72.
New Orleans, La., 24.
Newport County, R. I., 28.
Newport, R. I., 7, 8, 10, 11, 20, 21, 28, 29, 31, 34, 35, 39, 42, 47, 48, 49, 50, 51, 53, 55, 56, 57, 58, 68, 70.
New York, 5, 58.
North Kingstown, R. I., 35, 45.
Norwalk, Conn., 6.
Norwich, Conn., 10, 11.
"O'Larkin's Country," The, 48.
Orleans, Isle of, 21.
Oswego, N. Y., 49.
Paris, France, 55.
Pawtucket, R. I., 31.
Rawtuxet, R. I., 60, 63, 64, 68.
Pennsylvania, 6, 74.
Phenix, R. I., 24.
Philadelphia, Pa., 9, 10, 48, 54, 73, 74, 75.
Plymouth Colony, 4.
Plymouth, Mass., 4.
Point Judith, R. I., 70.
Portsmouth, N. H., 70.
Providence, R. I., 7, 8, 9, 10, 11, 19, 20, 21, 22, 25, 27, 29, 33, 34, 35, 36, 37, 38, 41, 44, 46, 47, 49, 50, 52, 53, 54, 59, 60, 63, 64, 65, 66, 67, 68, 69, 70, 72, 74.

Quebec, Can., 20, 21, 36.
Queen's County, Ire., 33.
Raphoe, Ire., 20.
Red Bank, 23.
Richmond, R. I., 40, 49.
Riverpoint, R. I., 22.
San Francisco, Cal., 47.
Saratoga County, N. Y., 32.
Savannah, Ga., 56, 57.
Scituate, R. I., 19.
Scotia Major, 37.
Scotia Minor, 37.
Scotland, 37, 69.
"Seacunnet," R. I., 33.
Sligo, Ire., 37.
Strabane, Ire., 73.
Swanzey, Mass., 68.
Thomastown, Ire., 29.
Ticonderoga, 47.
Tiverton, R. I., 23, 27, 42, 65, 68.
Ulster, Ire., 6, 69.
Valley Forge, Pa., 65.
Virginia, 4, 5, 6, 74.
Warren, Mass., 66.
Warren, R. I., 13, 31, 32, 33, 39, 40, 42, 68.
Warrenstown, Ire., 33.
Warwick, R. I., 24, 25, 31, 67, 68.
Waterford, Ire., 5, 28, 29, 33, 54.
Westchester County, N. Y., 23.
West Indies, 4, 5, 6.
Westmeath, Ire., 57.
West Point, N. Y., 46, 54.
West Springfield, Mass., 65.
Westerly, R. I., 20, 49.
Wethersfield, Conn., 72.
Wexford, Ire., 5, 73.
Weymouth, Mass., 63.
Youghal, Ire., 5.
Yorktown, 50, 55, 58.

AN INDEX OF NAMES.

Aborn, 24.
Alexander, 43.
Allen, 47.
Allin, 20, 31.
Almy, 56.
Amory, 10, 11.
Angell, 23, 27, 35, 41, 43, 44, 45, 47, 49, 50, 54.
Armstrong, 65.
Arnold, 7, 20, 21, 22, 29, 73.

Bagley, 13, 49.
Baker, 13, 32.
Barns, 13, 33.
Barr, 13, 45, 61.
Barrett, 8, 13, 50, 61.
Barritt, 13, 20.
Barrey, 61.
Barry, 10, 13, 45, 73.
Bayley, 64.
Beamish, 3.
Bennett, 13, 26, 30, 43, 61.
Berkeley, 29.
Bicknell, 13.
Bishop, 13, 17, 28.
Black, 9, 13, 44.
Blake, 18, 61, 71.
Blanchard, 58.
Boone, 38.
Bourk, 8.
Bourke, 56.
Bowen, 18.
Boyd, 13, 31, 52, 71.
Boyle, 61.
Bradford, 4.
Brady, 72.
Brendan, 3.

Brown, 41, 61, 63.
Bruodin, 5.
Bryan, 13, 42.
Buckley, 13, 51, 72.
Burk, 13, 28, 29, 38, 52, 62, 63.
Burke, 13, 30, 39, 54, 73.
Burn, 13, 22.
Burns, 13, 22, 35, 43, 49, 50, 53, 61, 62.
Butler, 10, 13, 47, 50, 72.
Byrn, 8.
Byrne, 22.

Cain, 13, 49, 52.
Cane, 13, 62.
Capron, 13, 44.
Carey, 13, 27, 41, 72.
Carr, 18, 27, 39.
Carrell, 13, 20.
Carroll, 8, 13, 27, 73.
Carthy, 45.
Carty, 7.
Cary, 7, 13, 14, 40, 49, 62.
Casady, 62.
Casey, 6, 7, 14, 17, 31, 44, 47, 62, 64.
Cassady, 64.
Casside, 7.
Cassidy, 7.
Caton, 14, 49.
Cavan, 14, 50.
Cavenaugh, 8.
Chapman, 72.
Church, 28, 44.
Chastellux, 11.
Clark, 38.
Clarke, 14, 30, 47.

Cochran, 62, 71.
Cook, 62.
Cooke, 10, 11, 67.
Cole, 30, 32, 37.
Collins, 5, 50.
Columbus, 3.
Condon, 5.
Conery, 62.
Conley, 14, 27.
Conner, 7, 14, 20, 45, 62, 64.
Connolly, 62, 64.
Connor, 14, 52, 62, 64.
Conway, 14, 17, 22, 30, 62.
Cooney, 14, 47.
Corcoran, 14.
Cornell, 42, 53.
Cortland, 74.
Coursey, 7.
Cowell, 13.
Cowen. 14, 27, 36, 62, 64, 71.
Crane, 65.
Crary, 27, 30, 36, 41, 42, 43, 44, 46, 47.
Creed, 14, 46.
Cromwell, 5, 33.
Crou, 14, 28, 29.
Crowley, 62.
Cullen, 5.
Cummings, 18.
Cummins, 52.
Currey, 52.
Curry, 62, 71.
Cushing, 60.
Custis, 7.

Dailey, 7, 14, 17.
Daily, 14, 30, 47, 62.
Daley, 14, 62.
Darcy, 57.
Davis, 29, 65.
Dawley, 26, 38.
Day, 14, 51, 72.
Dearborn, 71.
DeLancey, 23.
Delaney, 7, 10.
Dempsey, 7.
Dermott, 8.

DeRoo, 3.
Deux Ponts, 11.
Devett, 7.
Dexter, 30, 39, 42.
Dillon, 33, 55, 56, 57, 58.
Doharty, 35.
Doherty, 14, 17, 35, 45, 50.
Donal, 14, 22.
Donnagan, 62, 65.
Donnelly, 8, 14, 45.
Donohoe, 8.
Donop, 22.
Donovan, 8, 14, 17.
Doolinty, 14, 28, 29.
Dorothy, 45.
Dorrance, 14, 17, 18, 19.
Dougherty, 14, 20.
Dowd, 14, 43, 52, 62.
Downing, 71.
Doyle, 7, 14, 17, 45, 52, 53, 72.
Doyne, 37.
Drake, 10.
Dring, 7, 18.
Driscoll, 22.
Driskel, 14, 41.
Driskill, 14, 22, 30, 34, 42, 49, 52, 62, 65.
Driskle, 50.
Dudingston, 9.
Dun, 37.
Dunn, 7, 14, 37, 62.
Dunne, 37.
Dunphy, 8, 14, 45.
Duyer, 45.
Dwyer, 8, 14, 45, 52.
Dyer, 22.

Eagan, 14, 17.
Edwards, 19.
Egan, 8.
Elliott, 22, 27, 30, 41, 44, 45.
Ennis, 14, 27.

Farrell, 7.
Fay, 62, 72.
Fee, 45.
Fellows, 64.

Fells, 4.
Felt, 5.
Fenner, 40.
Field, 4, 13, 29, 52.
Fitton, 54.
Fittsgereld, 66.
Fitz Gerald, 56, 62, 66.
Fitzgerald, 8, 14, 17, 35, 41, 42, 47.
Fitzgerold, 66.
Fitzgerrald, 14, 42.
Fitzgerrl, 62.
Fitzjerld, 66.
Fitz Jerrell, 66.
Fitzjerrill, 66.
Fitzpatrick, 8, 49.
Flannagan, 14, 17, 47.
Fling, 72.
Flynn, 8, 72.
Flood, 62, 68.
Ford, 18, 52, 62.
Forde, 14, 43.
Foster, 14, 17, 33, 54.
Fox, 18.
Foy, 14, 44.
Franklin, 7.
Frazer, 46.

Gaffery, 14, 47.
Gallagher, 7.
Galligher, 14, 41.
Galloway, 7.
Garey, 14, 20.
Garven, 70.
Geoghegan, 57, 58.
Gibbon, 49.
Gibbons, 14.
Gill, 65.
Gilligan, 62, 66.
Gillpatrick, 61, 62.
Gilmore, 70, 72.
Gilpatrick, 49, 61, 62.
Ginness, 62.
Gleason, 62, 71.
Gleeson, 14, 26.
Glover, 45, 46.

Gowen, 68.
Gorman, 8.
Green, 26, 53.
Greene, 22, 23, 24, 25, 30, 31, 35, 37, 38, 39, 42, 44, 50, 67, 74, 75.
Griffen, 14, 42.
Griffin, 14, 26, 42, 50.
Griffis, 3.
Guild, 19.

Hackett, 14, 17, 46, 47, 70.
Hackmet, 14.
Hagerty, 14, 17, 20, 21.
Hale, 71.
Haley, 68.
Halley, 18.
Hammond, 64.
Hand, 10.
Haney, 14, 50.
Hanley, 8, 14, 26, 49, 50.
Hannington, 14, 20, 36.
Hany, 49.
Harrington, 14, 15, 36, 38, 40.
Hart, 15, 30, 50.
Hartagan, 8.
Harvey, 18, 45.
Hatch, 65.
Hawes, 64.
Hayden, 15, 20, 21, 27, 29, 47.
Hayes, 15, 34, 50.
Healey, 17, 29, 47.
Healy, 15, 29.
Hearn, 8.
Heath, 65.
Heffernan, 7, 52.
Heitman, 23.
Hendly, 15, 26, 34.
Hendricken, 29.
Henley, 50, 60.
Herrick, 15, 26.
Herrington, 38.
Hervey, 15.
Hickey, 8, 15, 20, 41.
Hicks, 15, 36.
Higgarty, 20.

Higgins, 7, 73.
Hines, 18.
Hinman, 37.
Hitchcock, 29, 30, 43.
Hodgkins, 46.
Hogan, 15, 17, 28, 50.
Hogen, 15, 45.
Holden, 31.
Hoppin, 22, 27, 30, 44.
Hopkins, 52.
Hotten, 4.
Howard, 66.
Howell, 44, 74.
Hoxsie, 37.
Hughes, 15, 17, 22, 23, 24, 25, 35.
Humphries, 27.
Humphry, 40.
Hurley, 7.
Huzzey, 15, 17, 34.

Irvine, 10.

Jackson, 15, 27, 29, 41, 48, 51, 60, 63, 64.
Jenckes, 73.
Johnson, 52, 71, 72.
Johnston, 43.
Jordan, 18, 62, 65.
Joyce, 3, 7, 15, 41, 46.

Kaine, 52.
Keef, 62.
Keene, 25.
Keeney, 72.
Keley, 62.
Kelley, 15, 31, 32, 34, 40, 42, 62, 68, 71.
Kelly, 7, 15, 17, 25, 26, 31, 32, 40, 47, 49, 50, 51, 54, 62, 70, 71.
Kenady, 15, 36.
Kenedy, 62, 72.
Keney, 62.
Kennady, 15, 36.
Kennedy, 15, 45, 47, 52, 53, 62.
Kennelly, 62.

Kenney, 63, 65, 71.
Kenny, 62, 65.
Killey, 15, 32, 34, 42, 52.
Kilmurray, 37.
Kimball, 44.
Kinady, 36.
King, 15, 18, 34.
Kirby, 15, 50.
Knox, 9, 10, 11, 15, 27, 62, 74.

Lacy, 58.
Lafayette, 45.
Lally, 57.
Lanahan, 8.
Lane, 62, 71.
Langdon, 70.
Larkin, 6, 7, 15, 17, 26, 46, 48, 52, 62.
Lary, 8, 71.
Latimer, 10.
Laval, 11.
Lawless, 7, 15, 30, 41, 47.
Leader, 5.
Lee, 7, 18, 52.
Lemasny, 15.
Lewis, 30.
Lingard, 6.
Linihan, 62.
Linniken, 7.
Lippincott, 3.
Lippitt, 22, 24, 25, 27, 30, 40, 47.
Long, 7, 15, 26, 27, 62.
Lowery, 15, 44.
Lovell, 65.
Lunt, 60.
Lynch, 55.
Lyon, 7, 15, 22, 60, 63.

Macarte, 7.
Macdonnall, 56.
Mack, 72.
Mackay, 15, 51.
Mackey, 7, 54.
Mackenzie, 69.
Mackown, 7.
Macoone, 7.

MacCarthy, 57.
MacCogan, 37.
MacDonnell, 37.
MacHugh, 37.
MacMahon, 58.
MacMallon, 32.
MacManus, 37.
MacMillen, 16, 32, 47.
MacMullen, 8, 32, 63.
MacMurray, 37.
MacSparran, 69.
McAfferty, 15, 50, 51.
McBride, 15, 63, 71.
McCaffray, 15, 36.
McCall, 15, 50.
McCane, 7.
McCartee, 15.
McCartel, 15, 36.
McCarthy, 7, 15, 17, 22, 45.
McCarty, 16, 45, 46, 58, 63, 71.
McCavney, 16.
McClary, 71.
McClenachan, 74.
McCloud, 15, 30.
McClure, 71, 72.
McCormick, 63.
McCoy, 16, 22, 30, 37, 45, 47, 52, 63, 71.
McCowan, 16, 36.
McCurtin, 63.
McDermit, 63.
McDermot, 16, 17.
McDermott, 56.
McDonald, 8, 16, 43.
McDonnell, 22.
McDonnold, 16, 50.
McDonold, 52.
McDonough, 56.
McElroy, 63.
McGee, 15, 71.
McGlaughlin, 63.
McGonegal, 7.
McGowan, 16, 43.
McGrath, 8, 16, 17, 51.
McGuire, 56.

McKean, 10.
McKown, 16, 46.
McLarey, 63.
McLaughlin, 16, 36.
McLouth, 16, 30, 44, 63.
McMickel, 63.
McMillan, 32, 71.
McMillion, 16, 32, 47.
McMilon, 16, 32.
McMullan, 16, 36.
McMurphy, 70.
McNamara, 16, 17, 36.
McNeal, 63.
M'Case, 16, 42.
M'Clanen, 16, 43.
Madden. 15, 35, 54, 63.
Magee, 8, 52.
Magennis, 56.
Maguire, 8.
Mahan, 63.
Mahoney, 8.
Mahony, 15, 35, 36.
Malavery, 7.
Mallon, 63.
Malone, 15, 51.
Maloney, 15, 17, 50, 72.
Manning, 15, 27, 49.
Martin, 7, 15, 27, 47, 52.
Mattison, 40.
Mawney, 8.
Mead, 52.
Mease, 73.
Melally, 53.
Melona, 72.
Meloney, 16.
Melony, 50, 63.
Miles, 72.
Miller, 16, 17, 33, 35.
Millerd, 43.
Mitchell, 7, 16, 30, 49, 50, 71.
Molloy, 68.
Monks, 16, 17, 35.
Montgomery, 20.
Montlezun, 55.
Moran, 16, 39.

Mooney, 70, 71.
Moore, 27, 31, 41, 50, 52, 63, 70, 71.
Morrigan, 16.
Morris, 16, 30, 39, 45, 47.
Morrison, 16, 35, 72.
Mountjoy, 7.
Moylan, 10.
Mulholland, 7.
Mullally, 53.
Mullen, 8, 16, 17, 45.
Mullens, 56, 57.
Mulligan, 16, 17, 20, 51.
Mullins, 57.
Mumford, 57.
Murfee, 16, 22, 30, 47.
Murfey, 16, 44.
Murfy, 44.
Murphy, 6, 7, 8, 16, 17, 26, 51.
Murray, 7, 8, 16, 30, 37, 44.
Murrey, 44.

Nagel, 43.
Nagle, 16, 43, 44.
Neal, 68, 71.
Nichols, 69, 71.
Nightingale, 37.
Nixon, 10.
Noonen, 16.
Norton, 16, 30.
Nunn, 19.

Obrian, 16, 39.
Obryan, 60, 63.
Olcott, 72.
Olney, 23, 30, 35, 38, 43, 44, 49, 50, 51.
Ormsbee, 32.
Otway, 3.
O'Brian, 16, 39, 40, 60, 63.
O'Briant, 16, 33.
O'Brien, 8, 16, 17, 32, 33, 39, 40, 57, 58.
O'Brient, 33, 40.
O'Bryan, 16, 40, 60, 72.
O'Bryant, 60, 63.
O'Byrne, 33.

O'Callaghan, 55, 56.
O'Carroll, 37, 56.
O'Conner, 68.
O'Connor, 56.
O'Daniel, 16, 29.
O'Daniels, 60, 63.
O'Donnell, 22.
O'Donoghue, 3.
O'Dougherty, 33.
O'Dunn, 37.
O'Farrell, 57.
O'Fay, 37.
O'Flannagan, 56.
O'Harra, 7, 16, 39.
O'Hart, 33.
O'Hurley, 56.
O'Kelley, 16, 32.
O'Kelly, 17, 56.
O'Larkin, 48.
O'Mahoney, 56.
O'Moran, 57, 58.
O'Muireadhaigh, 37.
O'Murray, 37.
O'Neal, 16, 17, 50.
O'Neil, 8, 56.
O'Neill, 56.
O'Reilly, 37.
O'Rourke, 37.
O'Sullivan, 10, 56.

Parker, 16, 17, 28, 39, 41.
Patrick, 4, 16, 49.
Patton, 10.
Peabody, 71.
Peck, 30.
Pendleton, 42.
Phelan, 60, 63.
Phelon, 7, 46, 60, 63.
Pierce, 46, 65.
Pigot, 32.
Pike, 64.
Pomeroy, 72.
Poor, 64.
Powers, 16, 26, 50.
Pray, 61.
Prendergast, 5.

Quigley, 72.
Ragen, 16, 49.
Raney, 72.
Rany, 27.
Ray, 16, 27, 52.
Read, 16, 47, 51.
Ready, 16, 51.
Reed, 72.
Reilly, 56.
Reily, 17, 47, 54.
Reynolds, 16, 27, 71, 73.
Richmond, 27, 36.
Riley, 17, 41, 72.
Roatch, 6, 8, 52.
Robertson, 7.
Robinson, 10.
Rochambeau, 11, 56, 57.
Rohan, 8.
Rogers, 64.
Ross, 17, 46.
Rourk, 7.
Ryan, 8, 20.
Ryand, 20.
Ryley, 52.

Sarsfield, 58.
Sayles, 38, 44.
Scammon, 61.
Schirmer, 3.
Scott, 71.
Ségur, 55.
Sellick, 5.
Sessions, 8, 20, 21, 68.
Shay, 7.
Shean, 61, 63.
Shee, 56.
Sheehan, 8.
Sheldon, 38.
Sheppard, 64.
Sherburn, 27, 44.
Sheridan, 56.
Shield, 49.
Shields, 17.
Sibsie, 4.
Smith, 17, 39, 41, 43, 44, 65, 66.
Sprague, 36, 41.

Spencer, 67.
Stack, 56.
Staples, 74.
Stark, 69, 70.
Stafford, 49.
St. Clair, 60.
Sterling, 8, 9, 17, 19, 20.
Stevens, 65.
Stewart, 10, 18, 27.
Stone, 51, 55, 57, 58.
Strange, 18, 52.
Stuart, 33.
Sullivan, 7, 9, 10, 11, 17, 21, 22, 37, 43, 45, 46, 50, 59, 61, 63, 67, 68, 69, 71, 74.
Sweeney, 52.

Taaffe, 56.
Tally, 8.
Tate, 71.
Taylor, 54.
Thayer, 20, 21, 29, 36, 64.
Thebaud, 5.
Thompson, 10.
Throope, 44.
Topham, 20, 27, 28, 38, 42, 44, 47.
Tracy, 6, 17, 20, 21, 45.
Tuley, 17, 49.
Tyler, 65, 72.

Varnum, 46, 53.
Vaughan, 18.
Vernon, 5.
Viomesnil, 56.
Vose, 60, 64, 65.

Wade, 61.
Wall, 17, 27.
Walpole, 5.
Walsh, 55.
Wanton, 8, 12.
Ward, 20.
Warren, 33.
Washington, 7, 9, 10, 20, 57, 67, 68, 75.
Watson, 17, 35.

Wayne, 10.
Webb, 3, 72.
Welch, 6, 17, 20, 37, 51, 52, 61, 71.
Welsh, 26.
West, 40.
Whalen, 17, 51.
Whelan, 25, 58.
Whelen, 7.

Whellon, 17, 51.
Whelon, 51.
Whipple, 30, 43.
Wigglesworth, 66.
Williams, 5.
Wilson, 17, 28.
Winthrop, 4.
Woodbury, 65.
Wright, 17, 33, 50.

PAPERS BY THOMAS HAMILTON MURRAY, RELATING TO RHODE ISLAND.

Reminiscences of Life along Narragansett's Shores (Providence, R. I., 1890).

Rambles in Rhode Island's South County (Providence, 1891).

Some Early Irish Members of the Society of Friends in Rhode Island (Providence, 1894).

The Dorrance Purchase—A Leaf from Rhode Island History (Boston, Mass., 1895).

The Irish Chapter in the History of Brown University (Providence, 1896).

The Irish Soldiers in King Philip's War—Including Reference to the "Great Swamp" Fight (New York city, 1896).

Five Colonial Rhode Islanders (Providence, 1897).

Early Irish Schoolmasters in Rhode Island (Washington, D. C., 1898).

Rev. James MacSparran, Irishman, Scholar, Preacher, and Philosopher, 1680-1757 (Boston, 1900).

[Over]

Matthew Watson, An Irish Settler of Barrington, R. I., 1722 (Boston, 1900).

The Romance of Sarah Alexander—Mother of Commodore O. H. Perry (New York city, 1901).

Charles MacCarthy, A Rhode Island Pioneer, 1677 (Somerset, O., 1901).

Thomas Casey of Ireland and Rhode Island, 1636-1719 (Boston, 1901).

Gen. John Sullivan, and the Battle of Rhode Island (Providence, 1902).

OTHER PAPERS BY MR. MURRAY.

The Libraries of Boston: Public, Semi-public, and Private (Boston, Mass., 1882).

The Old Schoolmasters of Boston (Boston, 1884).

The Mason Name in New England History (Boston, 1884).

The Thayers in America (Boston, 1884).

A Nation's Individuality (Boston, 1888).

The Irish Element in the State of Connecticut (Boston, 1888).

From Dawn to Revolution (Boston, 1889).

Thirty Historic American Families (Boston, 1889).

Concerning the McGuinness, McGinnis, Name (Providence, R. I., 1895).

The Dunlevy Family in Irish History, Mention of the Clan's Patrimony in Old Ulidia (Lawrence, Mass., 1895).

David O'Killia [O'Kelly], The Irishman; A Pioneer Settler at Yarmouth, Mass., as Early as 1657 (Boston, 1895).

The Dempsey Name, Old and Puissant (Denver, Col., 1896).

The Irish Morrisons; Eminent in Ancient Mediæval, and Modern Times. A Glance at the Origin of the Clan Name, Together with Reference to the Family's Patrimony in the Ancient Kingdom of Connacht (Lawrence, Mass., 1896).

The First Regiment, Pennsylvania Line (Philadelphia, 1896).

Some Patricks of the Revolution (New York city, 1896-'97).

No Entangling Alliance with England (Albany, N. Y., 1898).

The Objections to an Anglo-American Alliance (Boston, 1898).

Some Facts Concerning the Irish Washingtons (Boston, 1898).

The French Chapter in American History (Boston, 1899).

The Irish at Bunker Hill, 1775 (Boston, 1900).

The Moss Gatherers of Scituate, Mass (New York city, 1900).

Paul Revere *vs*. The King (Boston, 1901).

A Point Made Clear—The Brecks of Dorchester, Mass. (Boston, 1901).

Irish Settlers, Previous to 1742, in Portsmouth, N. H. (Boston, 1901).

Early Irish in the Plymouth Colony (Boston, 1901).

The Story of Miss Fitzgerald (Boston, 1901).

The Voyage of the Seaflower—from Ireland to Boston—1741 (Boston, 1902).

A Glance at the Vanguard—Irish Pioneers in Colonial Massachusetts (Boston, 1902).

Hugh Gaine, Irishman, New York Publisher, 1752–1809 (Boston, 1902).

Richard Dexter, A Forgotten Irish Pioneer of Boston, 1641 (New York city, 1902).

The American not an "Anglo-Saxon" People (Boston, 1902).

Early Irish Educators of American Youth (San Francisco, Cal., 1902).

The Nationality of Michael Bacon, a Pioneer of Dedham, Mass. (Dedham, 1902).

www.ingramcontent.com/pod-product-compliance
Lightning Source LLC
Chambersburg PA
CBHW070324100426
42743CB00011B/2549